Juvenile Instructor Office

Helpful Visions

designed for the instruction and encouragement of young Latter-day

Saints

Juvenile Instructor Office

Helpful Visions
designed for the instruction and encouragement of young Latter-day Saints

ISBN/EAN: 9783337335946

Printed in Europe, USA, Canada, Australia, Japan

Cover: Foto ©Lupo / pixelio.de

More available books at **www.hansebooks.com**

HELPFUL

VISIONS.

THE FOURTEENTH BOOK OF THE

FAITH-PROMOTING SERIES.

———•▶▶◀◀•———

Designed for the Instruction and Encouragement of
Young Latter-day Saints.

———◆●◆———

JUVENILE INSTRUCTOR OFFICE,,

SALT LAKE CITY, UTAH.

1887.

COMBINED
FAITH-PROMOTING
SERIES,

Nos. 1-5,   - - - - - - - - $1.35,

Nos. 6-10,   - - - - - - - - $1.25.

CONTENTS.

CHAPTER II.

CHAPTER III.

CHAPTER IV.

CHAPTER V.

TRAITORS.

PREFACE.

THE very encouraging reports we are constantly receiving from various parts of the country concerning the vast amount of good accomplished by these small publications, induces us to issue the fourteenth book, with the sincere hope that it may not be less interesting or instructive than those which have preceded it.

The Visions here recorded will again prove that truth is stranger than fiction, and we trust that a perusal of these manifestations will lead our young people to seek for the guidance of the Lord in all things, and make Him their constant friend. The article on traitors is very appropriate reading matter for the present season, and will, it is hoped, cause everyone to look upon the men of this class with the contempt they so justly merit, and sustain everyone in shunning as they would poison, any traitorous act.

Our great desire is that this little book may assist in the education and elevation of the young people and others who may peruse it.

THE PUBLISHERS.

A TERRIBLE ORDEAL.

BY O. F. WHITNEY.

CHAPTER I.

REMARKABLE SPIRITUAL MANIFESTATIONS—THRILLING
EXPERIENCE OF ELDER DAVID P. KIMBALL, AS NAR-
RATED BY HIMSELF.

THE following narrative of the experience of the late David
Patten Kimball, who was lost on the Salt River desert, Arizona, in the latter part of November, 1881, is taken by permission from a letter written by him to his sister, Helen Mar
Whitney, of this city, on the 8th of January, 1882. Brother
Kimball was then a resident of Jonesville, or Lehi, three
miles from Mesa, where the letter was written. The events
described took place while he was returning home from a trip
to Prescott, the capital of that Territory.

The experience related was of so remarkable a character as
to meet with dubiety on the part of some, especially those
inclined to be skeptical regarding spiritual manifestations.
Some went so far as to ascribe the sights and scenes through
which the narrator claimed to have passed, to the fevered
fancy of a mind disordered by strong drink. That such should
have been supposed, particularly by those who are ignorant of
spiritual things, is not surprising, when it is remembered that
even the Apostles of Christ, on the day of Pentecost, were

accused of being "drunken with new wine," when the power of the Spirit fell upon them and they "spake with tongues and prophesied."

What is here presented is the plain and simple testimony of an honest man, who adhered to it till the day of his death, which occurred within two years from the date of his letter, and was in literal fulfillment of certain things which he said were shown him in vision, and of which he frequently testified while living.

For the benefit of such as may not have known Brother David P. Kimball, we will state that he was the fourth son of the late President Heber C. Kimball, whose wonderful encounter with evil spirits, on the opening of the British Mission in 1837, has become a matter of Church history. Here is the excerpt from David's letter:

"On the 4th of November, I took a very severe cold in a snow storm at Prescott, being clad in light clothing, which brought on pneumonia or lung fever. I resorted to Jamaica ginger and pepper tea to obtain relief and keep up my strength till I could reach home and receive proper care. On the 13th I camped in a canyon ten miles west of Prescott, my son Patten being with me. We had a team of eight horses and two wagons. That night I suffered more than death. The next night we camped at Mr. McIntyre's, about twenty miles farther on. I stopped there two nights and one day, during which time I took nothing to drink but pepper tea. On the 16th we drove to Black's ranch, twenty-eight miles nearer home, and were very comfortably located in Mr. Black's house.

"About 11 p. m., I awoke and to my surprise saw some six or eight men standing around my bed. I had no dread of them but felt that they were my friends. At the same time I heard a voice which seemed to come from an eight square (octagon) clock on the opposite side of the house. It commenced talking and blackguarding, which drew my attention, when I was told to pay no attention to it. At this point I heard the most beautiful singing I ever listened to in all my life. These were the words, repeated three times by a choir:

'God bless Brother David Kimball.' I at once distinguished among them the voice of my second wife, Julia Merrill, who in life was a good singer. This, of course, astonished me. Just then my father commenced talking to me, the voice seeming to come from a long distance. He commenced by telling me of his associations with President Young, the Prophet Joseph, and others in the spirit world, then enquired about his children, and seemed to regret that his family were so scattered, and said there would be a great reformation in his family inside of two years. He also told me where I should live, also yourself and others, and a great many other things. I conversed freely with father, and my words were repeated three times by as many different persons, exactly as I spoke them, until they reached him, and then his words to me were handed down in a like manner.

"After all this I gave way to doubt, thinking it might be only a dream, and to convince myself that I was awake, I got up and walked out-doors into the open air.

"I returned and still the spirit of doubt was upon me. To test it further I asked my wife Julia to sing me a verse of one of her old songs. At that, the choir, which had continued singing, stopped and she sang the song through, every word being distinct and beautiful. The name of the song was, 'Does He Ever Think of Me.'

"My eyes were now turned toward the south, and there, as in a large parquette, I beheld hundreds, even thousands, of friends and relatives. I was then given the privilege of asking questions and did so. This lasted for some time, after which the singing commenced again, directly above me. I now wrapped myself in a pair of blankets and went out-doors, determined to see the singers, but could see nothing, though I could hear the voices just the same. I returned to my couch and the singing, which was all communicative and instructive, continued until the day dawned. All this time the clock I have mentioned continued its cursing and blackguarding.

"Mr. and Mrs. Black were up in due time and got breakfast. I arose and made my toilet, plain as it was, and took breakfast with my host and hostess. When my boy got ready to start, I went to pay my bill, and to my surprise heard a voice say or communicate: 'David Kimball has paid his bill.' When I got into the wagon, my guards, or those who were around my bed during the night, were still with me. My father had told me that he and President Young and others would visit me the next night.

"We drove on until about 11 a. m., when a host of evil spirits made their appearance. They were determined to destroy me, but I had power of mind to pay no attention to them, and let them curse all day without heeding them any more than possible. Five times they made a rush *en masse* to come into the wagon, the last one, where I was, but were kept off by my friends (spiritual). About 2 p. m. I told my boy to stop and we would water our horses. We used for this purpose barrels that we had along with us. After this I walked to the west side of my wagons, and looking to the east, I saw and heard the evil spirits floating in the air and chanting curses upon Brigham Young. I saw two other groups of the same kind, but did not hear them. Then I looked to the south and the whole atmosphere was crowded with fallen spirits, or those who had not obtained bodies. Others who tried to torment me were spirits who had lived upon the earth. Having seen so many and being complimented by my guard for seeing so well, I became a little timid and asked my spiritual friends if they had any help. The answer was, 'Yes, plenty.' I now told my boy to drive on—he was entirely oblivious of all that was taking place with me—and. soon after I was so exhausted that I fell into a troubled sleep and must have slept quite a little while.

"After I awoke I seemed to be left alone, and was lying on my back, when, all at once, I saw an old man and two young girls. This vision coming on me so suddenly, I was startled, and finding my guard gone, I jumped out of the wagon and got up on the spring seat beside my boy. But I could not get away from them. I was told in a coarse, gruff voice that the devil was going to kill me, and that he would follow me night and day until he destroyed me. I remembered the promise father had made me the night before—that he intended to visit me the next evening—and I nerved up and tried to pay no attention to my persecutors, but I must confess I was frightened.

"We arrived at Wickenburg just at sundown. The old man and the girls were tormenting and tantalizing me all the way, but never coming very near to me. We got supper and I took a room at Peeple's hotel and retired about 10 p. m. When everything was quiet my spirit friends, eight in number, returned and my tormentors were required to leave. Soon after, a glorious vision burst upon me. There were thousands of the Saints presented to me, many who had died at Nauvoo, in Winter Quarters, on the plains and in Utah.

"I saw Brother Pugmire and many others whom I did not know were dead. When my mother came to me it was so real and I was so overjoyed that I exclaimed aloud. So powerful was this vision that I asked President Young, who seemed to be directing matters, three times to relieve me, or I would faint. A great many others passed in regular order; and I recognized nearly all of them, and was told the names of all I did not know. My father sat in a chair with his legs crossed and his hands clasped together, as we have often seen him. Those who passed along had hidden him from my view till then.

"This scene vanished, and I was then taken in the vision into a vast building, which was built on the plan of the Order of Zion. I entered through a south door and found myself in a part of the building which was unfinished, though a great many workmen were busy upon it. My guide showed me all through this half of the house, and then took me through the other half, which was finished. The richness, grandeur and beauty of it defied description. There were many apartments in the house, which was very spacious, and they differed in size and the fineness of the workmanship, according to the merits on earth of those who were to occupy them. I felt most at home in the unfinished part, among the workmen. The upper part of the house was filled with Saints, but I could not see them, though some of them conversed with me, my father and mother, Uncle Joseph Young and others.

"My father told me many things, and I received many reproofs for my wrong-doings. Yet he was loth to have me leave, and seemed to feel very badly when the time came for me to go. He told me I could remain there if I chose to do so, but I plead with him that I might stay with my family long enough to make them comfortable, to repent of my sins, and more fully prepare myself for the change. Had it not been for this, I never should have returned home, except as a corpse. Father finally told me I could remain two years, and to do all the good I could during that time, after which he would come for me; he mentioned four others that he would come for also, though he did not say it would be at the same time.

"On the 18th of November, about noon, we left Wickenburg (which is twenty-two miles from Black's Ranch where we stopped the previous night) on our journey home. I was exhausted from what I had experienced, and could feel my mind fast giving away, but I had confidence that I would reach home alive. There were no Elders to administer to me and no kind friends to look after my wants except my son, who had all he could do in looking after eight horses and two wagons. As my mind wandered and grew weaker, I was troubled and led by influences over which I had no power, and my friends, the good spirits, had all left me.

"We drove about twenty miles that afternoon, camping about eight miles from water, on the Salt River desert, which is about fifty miles across. During the fore part of the night I heard the horses running as though they were frightened. My son was asleep, but I got up and put my overcoat across my shoulders and went out where they were and got them quieted down. I was about to return to the wagon, when that same old man with gray whiskers, who had tormented me before, stepped between me and the wagons. He had a long knife in his hand. I was frightened and fled, he pursuing me and telling me he was going to kill me. What I passed through I cannot describe, and no mortal tongue could tell. I wandered two days and three nights in the Salt River desert, undergoing the torments of the damned, most of the time, which was beyond anything that mortal could imagine.

"When my mind was restored, and the fever which had raged within me had abated, I found myself lying on a bleak hill-top, lost in the desert, chilled, hungered, thirsty and feeble. I had scarcely any clothing on, was barefooted, and my body full of cactus from head to foot. My hands were a perfect mat of thorns and briars. This, with the knowledge that no one was near me, made me realize the awful condition I was in. I could not walk. I thought I would take my life, but had no knife or any thing to do it with. I tried to cut an artery in my arm with a sharp rock I had picked up, hoping I might bleed to death, but even this was denied me. The wolves and ravens were hovering around me, anxiously awaiting my death. I had a long stick and I thought I would dig a deep hole and cover myself up the best I could, so the wolves would not devour my body until I could be found by my friends.

"On the night of the 21st, I could see a fire about twenty-five miles to the south, and felt satisfied that it was my friends coming after me. I knew the country where I was; I was about eight miles from houses where I could have got plenty of water and something to eat, but my strength was gone and my feet were so sore I could not stand up. Another long and dreary day passed, but I could see nothing but wolves and ravens and a barren desert covered with cactus, and had about made up my mind that the promise of two years life, made by my father, was not to be realized. While in this terrible plight, and when I had just about given up all hope, my father and mother appeared to me and gave me a drink of water and comforted me, telling me I would be found by my friends who were out searching for me, and that I should live two years longer as I had been promised. When night came I saw another fire a few hundred yards from me and could see my friends around it, but I was so hoarse I could not make them hear. By this time my body was almost lifeless and I could hardly move, but my mind was in a perfect condition and I could realize everything that happened around me.

"On the morning of the 23rd, at daylight, here they came, about twenty in all, two of my own sons, my nephew William,

Bishop E. Pomeroy, John Lewis, John Blackburn, Wiley
Jones and others, all friends and relatives from the Mesa, who
had tracked me between seventy-five and one hundred miles.
I shook hands with them, and they were all overjoyed to see
me alive, although in such a pitiable plight. My own feelings
I shall not undertake to describe. I told them to be very
careful how they let me have water, at first. They rolled me
up in some blankets and put me on a buck-board and appointed
John Lewis to look after me as doctor and nurse. After I had
taken a few swallows of water, I was almost frantic for more,
but they wisely refused to let me have it except in small doses
every half hour.

"I had about seventy-five miles to ride home. We arrived
at my place in Jonesville on the afternoon of the 24th of November, when my wife and family took charge of me and I was
tenderly and carefully nourished. In a few days I was around
again. I told my experience to President McDonald, Bishop
Pomeroy, C. I. Robson and others, and most of them believed
me, but my word was doubted by some. The report had gone
out that I had been drinking and was under the influence of
liquor. This was an utterly false report. I told them I had
just two years to live, so they could tell whether it was a true
manifestation or not.

"Now, Sister Helen, during the last twelve years I
have had doubts about the truth of 'Mormonism,' because I
did not take a course to keep my testimony alive within me.
And the letter I wrote you last August, I suppose caused you
to feel sorrowful, and you prayed for me and God heard your
prayers. And our father and mother plead with the Lord in
my behalf, to whom I will give the credit of this terrible but
useful ordeal through which I have passed and only in part
described, an ordeal which but few men have ever been able
to endure and relate what I have seen and heard.

"Now, my dear sister, you have a little of your brother
David's experience, and let who will think that I had been
drinking. I know these things were shown to me for my own
good, and it was no dream but a glorious and awful reality.
My story is believed by my brethren who have respect for me.

I will console myself with the knowledge I have obtained. Let the world wag on, and let hell and the devil keep up their warfare against the Saints of God. I know for myself that ''Mormonism'' is true. With God's help, while I live, I shall strive to do good, and I will see you before long and tell you all, as it never will be blotted out of my memory.

"With kind regards, in which my wife and children join, I remain, as ever,

Your Affectionate Brother,
David P. Kimball.''

———— •♦• ————

CHAPTER II.

ACCOUNT OF PATTEN KIMBALL AND OTHERS, REGARDING THE SEARCH FOR AND FINDING OF HIS FATHER.

THE following account is furnished by Elder Solomon F. Kimball, brother of David P. Kimball, who was in Mesa at the time of the occurrence described and thoroughly conversant with the facts:

On the morning of November 19th when Patten arose and missed his father he thought probably he had gone out to hunt for the horses, and felt no uneasiness concerning him. He made a fire, prepared breakfast and waited some time, but could not see or hear him anywhere. The horses came strolling into camp and were tied up, fed and watered. Patten then ate his meal and saddled a horse and rode back towards Wickenburg, until he came to a small place called Seymour on the Hassayampa but could find out nothing of his father's whereabouts. He went back to the wagon and hunted the country close around camp but found nothing but his father's overcoat, which was a few hundred yards from the wagon. It being an old camp-ground, it was impossible to find his tracks. He finally came to the conclusion that he had gone towards home,

so he hitched up his team and drove homeward until he came
to Mr. Calderwoods at Agua Fria. (Cold Water). At this
place there was a well dug on the desert about twenty miles
from Salt River. Patten had traveled about twenty-two miles
before reaching this point, but was disappointed in not hearing
anything of his father. He had traveled all night and Mr.
Calderwood was up and around when he arrived. He related
his story to him and was advised by him to leave his team
there and take the best pair of horses, and hitch them to his
buck-board and go on to the Mesa. Here he could get help
to come and hunt for the missing man. The distance was
forty miles, which would take all the rest of the day (the 20th).
He acted on the advice, however, and arrived at his destination at 9 p. m. The news was circulated, and in less than
two hours, twenty of the best and most experienced men at
Mesa and Jonesville were on the road, taking Patten back with
them. They also took a wagon to carry water and provisions,
but most of them were on the best of horses. They had sixty
miles to ride, before beginning the search, which was accomplished by daylight next morning. After feeding their horses
and eating a lunch they held a consultation and agreed to abide
by the following rule. If any one of the party found his
tracks he was to make a smoke and this would call the others
in that direction. They then started out in different directions.
They scoured the country until about noon, when Sern Sorn-
son and Charles Rogers found his tracks. They supposed
they were about twelve miles from where he was lost, and about
ten miles from Agua Fria, close to the main road on the south
side. They soon gathered some brush and started a fire, putting on plenty of green weeds, etc., to cause a smoke, and soon
attracted the attention of their comrades. His tracks were
followed. They wound round and round, going in no particular direction. Some places he would cross his tracks eight
or ten times in going one hundred yards, which made it quite
difficult to follow.

After spending a part of the afternoon trailing him up, the
tracks finally took a direct course leading to the north. By
this time all the searching party were together.

Another meeting was held and the plan adopted was for eight horsemen, four on each side of his tracks, to ride at a considerable distance apart, so as to cut off the track if it turned to the right or left, and two or three of the best trailers to keep on the tracks, while the buck-board and wagon followed up. These were out of sight most of the time, as very good time was made by the trailers after this plan was adopted. The ground was quite soft, and those on the trail would gallop their horses for miles, but darkness soon put an end to their work for this day, a good thing for both men and animals.

They had traveled upwards of one hundred miles in about twenty hours. They were working men and had plenty of strength to carry them through under all circumstances. They camped on the highest ground that could be found close by, and made a large fire which was kept up all night by those on guard.

As soon as it was light enough to see the tracks, every man was at his place moving as fast as he could under the circumstances.

This was the morning of the 22nd. One great drawback they met with that day was that when they would come to a deep ravine where water had run during rainy weather, the tracks would follow up sometimes for miles and then continue in the former direction. Places would frequently be found in the sand where the lost one had dug down for water with his hands. Now and then they would find a piece of his clothing and see places where he had run into the fox-tail cactus, cat's-claw and other thorny bushes. One place was found where he had broken off the limb of a tree for a walking stick. The party followed his tracks all day without stopping, only as they were obliged to, on account of losing the trail or from some other cause.

Darkness overtook them again, but nothing could be heard or seen of the missing man. They slept on his tracks, keeping up a fire all night as before. His sons and others could not rest, and followed his tracks after dark by striking matches and putting them close to the ground to see if they might possibly find him. Some thought they could hear a sound but it was so indistinct they could not discern the direction from which it came. It was indeed he who called, for they were then only a few hundred yards from him, but he was too hoarse to make them hear. On the morning of the 23rd at daylight his anxious friends were on his tracks, and had gone but a short distance when Charles Peterson saw him. He had a long staff in his hand, and had raised up as high as he could get, being on one knee and the other foot on the ground, and was stretching himself as far as he could and looking eagerly for their arrival. The crowd made a rush, and in a few seconds were with him, Bishop E. Pomeroy being the first. He was in his right mind and knew all present, and was glad to shake them by the hand, calling each by name. He was in good spirits and joked the boys frequently and gave them instructions to be careful in giving him water, etc. There was no water except in a canteen that had been reserved for his especial use. The company suffered themselves for want of water. They had traveled upwards of one hundred and fifty miles in less than forty-eight hours.

David had dug a deep hole with his stick and had used his hands to move the dirt. He said he was digging his own grave. He was rolled in blankets and put on the buck-board. All drove to the nearest houses, seven or eight miles distant, on the Hassayampa, where all refreshed themselves with water and something to eat. Soon they were on the road homeward. They drove to Mr. Calderwood's, which was about thirty miles, and stayed all night. He was very kind to all and told them to help themselves to any thing he had, such as hay, grain and food. He acted the gentleman in every respect. A large number of men had also left Phœnix in search of David, among them being the U. S. Marshal, and others. Men and Indians were riding over the desert in every direction. Next morning the company drove to Jonesville, forty miles distant, where they arrived about 3 p. m.

David was carried into his house where he was surrounded by his loving wife and children.

When he recounted his experience, he said that one thing that kept him from choking to death for want of water, was the damp pebbles which he dug from low ravines and held them in his mouth. The Indians said that no human being could walk as far as he did, go without water and live four days and five nights. The party that found him said he must have walked at least seventy-five miles, some said one hundred.

He testified that on the afternoon of the 22nd, his father and mother came and gave him water and told him that his friends would find him. His clothing was all gone except his under garments, which were badly torn.

Before leaving home on his trip to Prescott, David had worked several days fixing up his books and accounts, and burning up all useless papers, after which he told his wife that he felt different in starting on this trip from anything he had ever felt before. He said it seemed to him that he should never return. He told her that if this proved to be the case, he had fixed his business up in such a shape that she would have no trouble, and would know as much about it as himself. She frequently spoke of these curious remarks, and felt considerably worried. When the news came that he was lost, all was plain to her, and she never expected to see him come home alive. Nothing could comfort her and she watched night and day until he was brought home.

In the Fall of 1883, Elder David P. Kimball paid a visit to Salt Lake City, to see his sister Helen and others, to whom he confirmed by his own lips all that his letter contained, and told some other things in relation to his marvelous experience. He declared solemnly to her that he was perfectly sober when he passed through the trying ordeal related, and bore a powerful testimony to the truth of "Mormonism." He seemed a little reticent to most of his relatives, and talked but little of his strange experience, feeling pained that so many seemed to doubt his word, and being unwilling to make himself obtrusive. When he bade his friends farewell, there was something about him which seemed to say that he was taking leave of them for all time. This visit was no doubt made with that prospect, for it was almost two years from the time he was lost on the desert. He returned home to St. David, Cochise County, Arizona, and almost the next news that came from there was the tidings of his death.

A letter from his nephew, Charles S. Whitney, who was then living with him, written home on the 22nd of November, 1883, contained this:

"Uncle David died this morning at half-past six, easily, and apparently without a bit of pain. Shortly before he died, he looked up and called, 'Father, father!' All night long he had called for Uncle Heber. You remember hearing him tell how grand-pa came to him when he was lost on the desert, and how he plead for two more years and was given that much longer to stay. Last Saturday, the day he was so bad, was just two years from the day he was lost, and to-day is just two years from the day his father and mother came to him and gave him a drink of water, and told him that his friends would find him and he should live two years longer. He knew that he was going to die, and bade Aunt Caroline good-by day before yesterday."

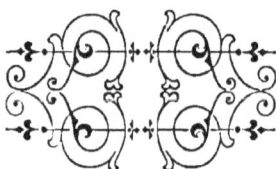

BRIANT S. STEVENS.

A Little Savior in the Midst of His
Young Companions.

BY KENNON.

\

CHAPTER I.

BRIANT STRINGAM STEVENS BECOMES A MISSIONARY TO HIS
ASSOCIATES AND BRINGS FOUR BOYS TO BELIEF AND
BAPTISM—A GOOD CHILD WHO PASSED AMIDST THE
DAILY TEMPTATIONS OF LIFE UNSCATHED.

"IF there is anything that will endure
    The eye of God because it still is pure,
It is the spirit of a little child,
    Fresh from His hands, and therefore undefiled.
Nearer the gate of Paradise than we,
    Our children breathe its airs, its angels see;
And when they pray God hears their simple prayer,
    Yea, even sheathes His sword, in judgment bare."

THESE thoughtful words of the poet always recurred to
my mind when I met little Briant Stevens. We
notice, with most children, how quickly they grow away
from the absolute and perfect purity of childhood into the
heedlessness of youth; and often, too often, with their experience of life comes experience of wrong. Of all the boys that
I ever met, who had reached years of accountability, I think
Briant Stevens bore in his face and manner the most evidence

of a retention of that saintliness which is the endowment of
each of God's little ones. Not that he seemed too solemn for
earth: but because there was a fearless grace, and yet a tenderness, which showed that the inherent beauty of his young life
was still unsoiled.

> "You hear that boy laugh?—you think he's in fun;
> But the angels laugh, too, at the good he has done;
> The children laugh loud as they troop to his ca'l,
> And the poor man that knows him laughs loudest of all!"

This was the boy, Briant Stringam Stevens. Often have I
seen strangers when passing him in the street pause and make
inquiry concerning him. His demeanor was so admirable that
they could not restrain a desire to know something of him.
Distinctly I can remember the first time I ever saw him—when
he was about ten years old. He had his books under his arm,
and was evidently going to school. His appearance was so
attractive that I felt impelled to stop him and ask his name.
Without the slightest embarrassment, he lifted his hat and
answered me politely and cordially. From that time I never
met him without receiving his gentlemanly salutation. Those
of our people who knew him can all conscientiously speak of
him as "The Little Saint;" scores of worldly people who knew
him call him "The Little Gentleman."

BRIANT STRINGAM STEVENS was the son of Thomas Jordan
Stevens and Maria Stringam Stevens, and the grandson of
Briant Stringam. He was born December 24th, 1873, in the
Thirteenth Ward of Salt Lake City. He died February 3rd,
1887, at Ogden.

Few people who have barely lived to enter their fourteenth
year have done so much that is worthy of record and emulation
as this little boy. After he had obtained membership in the
Church through baptism, he became deeply impressed with
the desire to bring the same blessings to others. Among his
playmates were several boys who were his own age and
some who were older than himself; and whose parents had
failed—either through carelessness or intention—to have their
children baptized. Without a hint from any person, little

Briant took upon himself the duty to convince these children and their parents of the necessity of bapti:m. What anxious hours the little fellow spent in devising means to influence his playmates, no one living now can tell; but the subject seemed ever present with him, and after months of labor among his companions he had converted four of the boys at least one of whom was older than himself, to a belief in the Gospel, and to desire for membership in the Church of Christ. Briant a-ked his father to administer the ordinance to these little converts; but Brother Stevens informed the child that he could not baptize any of the boys without the consent of their par nts. Still of his own volition, and without instruction or advice from anybody, Briant visited the homes of his playmates, and began a missionary labor with the parents. Nothing could discourage him; he went bravely to the people and pleaded with them on behalf of their sons.

And, after patient and hopeful waiting, Briant gained the consent which he so earnestly sought. It was a happy day for him when he went with his father to the bank of the Ogden River and saw his companions, who were most truly his little brethren, emerge from the water and receive their confirmation for the gift of the Holy Ghost.

But Briant's guardianship of these boys did not end when their baptism was accomplished. With a gravity beyond his years, he visited them one after another at their homes, and instructed them concerning the responsibilities which they had assumed, and the necessity of purity of conduct becoming to Saints of God, if they wished to derive blessing from their obedience to the holy requirement. Whenever and wherever he met them, he was always ready and able to counsel them; and yet he did not trouble them with long sermons, but spoke to them with so much feeling and good-fellowship that they were led day by day to a greater detestation of evil, and to a greater love for good.

He persuaded them to attend Sunday School, and to take part in the exercises of the Preceptor Class; never permitting them to wander very long or very far without giving them his admonition. Older persons who have had experience in this matter will readily understand that his work, even with his four young converts, was a daily one. It was not sufficient to bring them into the Church; but, with all the distracting influences which surrounded them, it was necessary that they should learn to love the truth and to understand it for themselves.

One of these boys, who lived near to Briant's home and was his frequent companion, became anxious to hold the Aaronic Priesthood. He had arrived at years which justified that wish, and he talked with Briant upon the subject. Briant consulted with Brother Stevens and learned that it would be possible for his companion to receive the desired ordinance, but that consent must be gained from the boy's parents. Again Briant took upon himself the responsibility of gaining that permission; but the opportunity did not come in this life.

He was extending his little missionary labors up to the very hour that he was stricken. Several other boys had aroused his interest, and sometimes he confided to his father that he hoped to see these companions do much good, though their ways were not always becoming to children who believed in the gospel. On more than one occasion when he found these boys lapsing into wrong-doing or carelessness, he confessed to his father a fear that he would not be able to do them any good, and that he must cease his association with them. And yet he always returned to the labor with renewed hope and courage.

It is a dangerous experiment to trust one good boy with a number of playmates who are not what they should be; because, as a rule, he learns to partake with them. But Brother Stevens gives a marvelous testimony to the worth of his son when he says:

"I never felt the slightest fear for Briant. In this matter I knew that he was led by a good Spirit, and I trusted him implicitly and without requiring him to account for his conduct. He seemed in all matters of goodness to be easily impressed; but evil appeared, if not incomprehensible, at least entirely unattractive to him."

The teacher of the Preceptor Class which Briant attended was Brother Austin C. Brown; he says that the questions which Briant propounded to him cccasioned great marvel in his mind. The clearness with which the young boy spoke of the principles of the gospel, the perfect understanding which he seemed to gain, almost intuitively, of the truth, were as surprising as they were gratifying. In other matters the boy was very precocious. He attended the academic department of the Central School of Ogden, and was the youngest, though not the last, in his class. He early developed a talent for drawing and painting, and his parents and friends are now in possession of some exquisite little gems produced by him.

Before he received the Priesthood he was a constant attend-ant upon the meetings of his young brethren, the Deacons; and he anxiously awaited the time when he could be deemed of sufficient age and worth to receive an ordination to this calling. He had the highest reverence for the Priesthood, and he believed most firmly in the power of the gospel. Whenever he was in pain or illness, his sole desire was for the blessing of his father or other Elders of the Church. Several times he was instantly healed from infirmities under the administration of the servants of God.

At home he was perpetual sunshine. From the hour that he was 10 years old he never permitted his father to attend to any of the labors in the garden or with the stock which his young hands could perform. He was so kind to the horse and the cow, and the other domestic animals, that they learned to know him and to love him perfectly. Even the cat would fol-low him through the garden, and run to rub her head against his leg. The parrot, when released from its cage, would fol-low him about the house like a dog. It would mount to his shoulder and kiss his cheeks or lips daintily and tenderly; while with everbody else it showed the crossness for which parrots are proverbial, biting, scolding and clawing at the slightest attempt at familiarity.

Briant kept many pigeons—often as many as fifty at one time. They knew him and flocked about him fearlessly. He gave many of them away to his young friends, but never with-out exacting a promise from the boys that they would be kind to the birds and would not sell them to anyone who would abuse them.   He had a great horror of the cruelty of pigeon-shooting matches, and would not sell one of his doves for such a purpose under any circumstances, or for any amount of money.   If strange boys came to him to buy pigeons, he invariably enquired for what purpose they were purchased. And unless the buyers would give him a faithful promise not to sell the birds for shooting-matches, he would not part with his pets.

Whenever he received money from the sale of pigeons, he carried it to his father, and offered it with the remark that he cared nothing for it, and wanted his father to use it for the best purpose.   He had but one extravagance with money—and that was to give it to the poor.   Not only would he part with his last dime for this purpose, but often he borrowed money from his relatives and friends to give to the needy.

About four years before Briant's death, his little brother, Jordan, died.   The two had been inseparable—brothers in the fullest sense.   They shared all their possessions equally; and one never felt content without the presence and happiness of the other.   When Jordan passed from earth, Briant said to his father:

"I know that my dear little brother is happy and well; but I cannot help feeling lonesome."

He gathered up Jordan's share of the toys and books which had belonged to them, and put them sacredly away.   To this hour they remain in the place and in the order where they were put by his loving little hands.

A few months before Briant was stricken he lost a favorite pigeon.   It was a snow-white bird which had belonged to Jordan.   When Briant found that it was surely gone he shed some tears, and said to his mother:

"I would have preferred to lose all my other pigeons than to have lost Whitey, for that was little Jordie's pet."

Then he drew a perfect picture of the lost bird and placed it in a nook in the barn, underneath these words:

"Whitey, nine years old."

With all the many virtues and the thoughtfulness of this little boy, he was not mawkish in his manner.   At times, when deeply impressed, he was solemn in word and look; but he was full of healthy sentiment, and was bubbling over with energy and brightness.

---◆●◆---

CHAPTER II.

ACCIDENTS TO BRIANT—HE IS ORDAINED TO THE PRIEST-
HOOD—PATIENT ENDURANCE OF HIS SUFFERINGS—
HE IS BLESSED TO BE AN ELDER AND THEN SLUMBERS
IN DEATH.

IN October last, 1886, with a number of companions Briant was playing on a trapeze at the house of a friend, when he fell and broke his right arm. Af er the accident, Briant did not hurry to his home, which was only a block away; but an hour later his father found him at the doctor's office, where the arm had been set. Briant was perfectly composed; and, instead of crying as most boys do when a new sympathiser comes, he gave his first thought to his mother, who had been quite ill and had not yet entirely recovered. He said to his father:

"I hope mamma does not know of this. If not, then we will keep it from her; because she would worry a great deal, and the anxiety might make her worse."

When they went home Briant bounded into the house with a smile on his lips, and in reply to his mother's anxious questions he said:

"Nothing serious, mamma. I have strained my arm; but it will be well in a few days."

He kissed her and then ran laughing from the room, although at the time he must have been suffering excruciating pain. Some time elapsed before his mother knew the truth; and then she did not learn it from Briant.

He had recovered from the outward appearance of his injury to his arm, but it was not yet strong, when he met with another and more serious accident. With two of his companions he was jumping from a low roof. when his foot caught and he fell headlong to the ground. The weak arm received the weight of the shock; the old break was re-opened and the bones were split in a new place, and one of them protruded from a bleeding wound in the wrist. He had fallen upon a heap of sand, and when he rose to his feet he found that in the gash made by the broken bone the sand and dirt had penetrated. He sat down and wiped his wrist and the bone clean, put back the bone inside the flesh of his arm, and then started for the doctor's office. As in the other instance, his home was only a block away, but he did not wish to alarm his folks. Failing to find the doctor he went to a drug store, and, explaining his injury, asked that the physician be sent for. An hour later Brother Stevens found Briant sitting, pale but complacent, in the doctor's office, awaiting treatment. The necessary operation was long and painful, and at its close Briant was very weak. He whispered to his father:

"I am all right, papa, and will soon be well; but I hope that we can get home quickly, because I want you to administer to me."

This second serious accident occurred on the 18th of January, 1887; a week later—on the 25th day of the month—lockjaw set in, and his suffering became intense.

Brother Stevens went on the day following to ask the assistance of Elders George W. Larkin and Moroni Poulter in watching with Briant; and these two brethren remained alternately at the child's bedside, day and night, until he closed his eyes in death. On the morning of the 26th of January, before the visit of Brother Stevens, Elder Larkin said to his family:

"I had a strange and sad dream about little Briant Stevens last night. I wonder if the boy is sick."

Half an hour later Brother Stevens called with the sorrowful message; but Elder Larkin, though amazed at the coincidence, would not relate the nature of his dream, for fear of rending the father's heart. But the dream was later fulfilled to the letter, and was then fully stated.

Bishop Stratford had selected Briant, a few weeks before the second accident, as a proper subject for ordination to the Aaronic Priesthood; but the ordinance had not yet been attended to. And while Briant was prostrated, he was comforted by receiving this blessing under the direction of the proper authorities. At the same time he remembered his promise to his young convert and companion, and he so impressed his anxiety upon his father's mind that—on the very day of Briant's funeral—Brother Stevens visited the other little chap and made an arrangement for his ordination.

When the more serious affliction of lock-jaw came upon Briant, he expressed but one regret: he feared that his misfortunes were bringing trouble and annoyance upon his parents and friends. Beyond this source of anxiety, all was peace with him. He never expressed the slightest fear for himself. He was always, according to his hopeful words, in a state of improvement: never needing anything except the blessing of God; never enduring much pain; but quite content if the Elders were present to administer to him and to talk with him about the things of God.

One day he called his father and mother to his bedside and said to them:

"I am not afraid to die; for there is nothing in death of which I have any dread. Only I want to take part in the building of the temple to God in Jackson County."

On another occasion he said to the Elders who were watching with him:

"I shall get better soon, and then I shall be able to repay you for your great kindness. I want to see the coming of our Lord Jesus; I want to go back to Jackson County to help to build the temple there for Him. And I know that I *will* aid in this work."

One of the brethren was moved upon by the Spirit of God to administer to Briant and to promise that this hope should be fulfilled; that the boy should see the coming of Christ and be with the Saints in Jackson County when they should build the temple.

Night after night the Elders came and watched with Briant, blessing him and ministering to his wants. They esteemed it not a task, but a pleasure; because, as they all stated, they never before felt such a constant power and influence of the

Spirit as they encountered at this boy's bedside. So peaceful and joyous was the manifestation to them that everyone felt that no death was in the house.

But the night before Briant died one of the Elders who had attended at the bedside, fell asleep while thinking about the sick child. He dreamed that himself and three of his companion Elders, who had also waited on Briant, went upon a journey into a distant and beautiful country. They seemed to have some definite object in view, but during their travel this object was not present to their minds.

When they reached the fair land of their destination, they saw a superb building, which they at once divined to be a temple of the living God. It was not yet completed; but it had assumed such proportions as to show the utmost grandeur. It was constructed of white, shining stone, seemingly as hard as granite. Many workmen appeared to be engaged in the building; and one of them, clothed in a white robe, with his head and hands and feet bare, stood upon the ground near the entrance to the structure.

In the white outer wall, at one side of the mighty arched doorway, and at the height of a man's head, a monogram seemed to be newly set into the stone. It was composed of three letters; the top one being B, clearly distinguishable; and the other two being fainter. At once the sojourners knew that this was what they had come after. The Elder who dreamed, thought that he reached forward and attempted to take it from its p'ace. But the white robed workman stayed his hand, saying:

"You cannot take it. It has been set here by order of the Master, as an ornament to this temple."

The Elders then walked around the building, and entered the interior through a magnificent portal, and saw that much workmanship of fine patterns was being used in the adornment of the structure. They walked out and once more essayed to pluck the monogram from its place in the glittering wall. But again the voice of the guardian workman stayed their hands. For the second time they walked around the temple, entered through the archway and gazed at the magnificent interior. Then they said: ·

"Let us try once more."

The third time the Elder stretched out his hand to take the monogram; but, as on the other occasions, he was told to desist. The workman had spoken to him each time in perfect kindness, but in a decided tone. On this final effort a voice sounding like a trumpet descended from the top of the building, saying:

"Brother [calling him by name], you must go back; your wish cannot be granted."

Then they withdrew. Soon the Elder awoke, and he felt certain that the prayers which had been offered concerning Briant Stevens—though they had reached the throne of the Eternal Father—were powerless to change the decree which had been made in heaven concerning the boy, and that Briant must speedily pass from earth.

The next day this Elder was sitting in Fast meeting, when the dream recurred to his mind; and instantly he felt that Briant should be ordained to the Melchisedec Priesthood before his death. The Elder would have gone to the house, but a sudden impression came to him that he need have no anxiety, for the matter was already receiving attention.

On the morning of the 3rd of February, which was Fast-day, Brother Stevens was prompted to ordain Briant to the Melchisedec Priesthood; but he endeavored to banish the thought from his mind. It constantly recurred to him, each time growing more imperative. He was not alone in this feeling, for several Elders who had watched with Briant felt the same influence at the same time, although they were not all present. But one of them, who was sitting at the bedside, said:

"Brother Stevens, I have felt for several hours that I ought to speak to you about ordaining Briant to be an Elder in the Church. I think that you ought to do this at once."

Brother Stevens admitted that the same feeling had been in his mind; but that he had hesitated, for fear that such a course might seem like giving up a hope of Briant's recovery. But after such admonitions he could no longer neglect the warning, and he sent for the Bishop. The messenger, on his

way to the Bishop's place, met President Shurtliff and spoke
to him of Briant; and the President seemed to have enter-
tained the same thought, for he said that he was led to believe
that Briant should receive the Melchisedec Priesthood.

When this holy ordination was conferred upon him, Briant
became serene, though he had been in great pain for some
time preceding, and he sank at once into an easy slumber.

He woke not in this world. In an hour his breathing
ceased and his spirit left the tortured clay to undergo the
transition of nature, while the noble life went to another realm
to perform its destined mission.

Elder George Larkin was in the room when Briant died;
and to him was entrusted the sad duty of preparing the wasted
body for its burial. When his solemn task was completed he
burst into tears and said to Brother Stevens:

"Now my dream is fulfilled. The night before you called
for me, a vision came in my slumber. I saw Briant lying dead
in this room, and mine was the dread duty to wash and dress
his deserted tabernacle and place it in the coffin. And so it
has come to pass, exactly according to my dream."

CHAPTER III;

A "HELPFUL VISION" TO BRIANT'S STRICKEN FATHER—
THE COMFORTER BRINGS THE PEACE WHICH PASSES
ALL UNDERSTANDING—THE FUNERAL OF THE LITTLE
MISSIONARY—HIS WORK LIVES AFTER HIM.

THERE was but one thought produced in the minds of all who
knew of the last scene at this good little Briant's bedside:
it was that in all the spasms and torture of his dread disease
he had been kept alive to receive the power of this ordination;
and as soon as the administration was effected, the purpose of
his mortal life was fulfilled, and he passed from a peaceful
slumber on earth into a glorious waking beyond.

The night after Briant died, Brother and Sister Stevens
were crushed with woe. They were not entirely disconsolate;

they did not mourn as those who have no hope, and yet they
seemed unable to reconcile themselves to the loss of their
pride and joy. Brother Stevens himself said to a friend at
this hour:

"I know that Briant is at peace. I know that he is a trea-
sure and a joy to his God wherever he is; and I do not repine
at the decree which has taken him away, after so many years
of blessing in his society; but when I remember that in every
nook about our home there is some evidence of his handiwork;
when I think of all the comfort he has been—I cannot hold
back this feeling of agony."

That night Brother Stevens prayed that the Lord would give
consolation and make manifest something of His glory
to banish the overwhelming sorrow which was in that stricken
home. When Brother Stevens fell asleep he dreamed; and it
became a dream within a dream:

He thought that he went to bed and dreamed that Briant
was dead. The friends and relatives who flocked around were
moaning in anguish and asking in agonized tones what they
could do to bring little Briant back to life. The father retired
to a room and fell upon his knees, and asked the Lord what
should be done in the matter; and the voice of the Spirit came
to him, saying:

"COVER BRIANT'S BODY WITH CLAY; AND THEN PATIENTLY
AWAIT MY PURPOSE. IF YOU WILL OBEY THIS COMMAND,
I WILL SHOW YOU THE GLORY NOW POSSESSED BY BRI-
ANT."

While he still knelt this command was repeated; and he
rose to his feet. Entering the room where the little white-
robed figure lay, he said to the weeping attendants:

"I know now what I shall do. You need worry no more;
because God has told me, and I will fulfill His design."

The father lifted the body in his arms from the bed whereon
it lay in dread repose, and laid it upon the floor. He took
clay and with his hands covered the marble form deeply,
until there was visible no semblance of the body. And
then he sat down to await God's purpose. A long time and
patiently he seemed to sit; and at length he saw a light and in

this light was little Briant, standing in the air, robed in snowy whiteness, with a face transfigured in its light and beauty. The boy smiled at him and moved his hands as if in loving recognition. This ethereal form of Briant moved about in the room without effort. A single inclination of the shining head seemed to project the body in any desired direction.

While the father watched and marvelled and felt great joy, he dreamed that he awoke from his dream and found his little Briant still convulsed and tortured by the power of the Destroyer.

And then he seemed to weep in agony because of his boy's suffering; for now instead of a familiar face yet transfigured in lovely happiness, he saw a countenance strange and distorted by pain. He wished and prayed that Briant's torture might cease, and that the boy might be translated to heavenly radiance.

But soon in reality the father awoke, and sensed that Briant was surely dead. And back came to his soul the feeling of patient hope and unrepining trust which had seemed to pervade the inner dream. He sincerely and submissively praised God's holy name. He told his wife what he had seen in this vision of the night, and together they took comfort; and through all the tribu'ation and loneliness which have followed the loss of their eldest boy, they have felt a comfort and sustaining power which nothing on earth can give, and nothing on earth can take away. They know that, having covered Briant's body with clay, they have now but to patiently await God's purpose, and He will sometime restore to them the glorified, the redeemed, the happy child.

The funeral of this little Elder of the Church was held in the Ward Meeting House in Ogden on Sunday, February 6th, 1887, and was attended by some hundreds of people, ten of Briant's young companions acting as pall-bearers.

It was the remark of the majority of those who were present that the Spirit of God seemed to fill the meeting-house and make its abiding-place in every heart. Among the speakers were the Elders who had attended Briant in his final act of suffering. They paid a glorious tribute to his patience and to his integrity. All felt that it was in fulfillment of God's own purpose that Briant had been called from earth; and that the agony which he had endured was but the doorway through which he entered into the Eternal Presence. The Elder who had promised in a holy administration to Briant that the child should have his hope fulfilled and engage in the building of the temple with the Saints in Jackson County, addressed the congregation in a most feeling manner. It was he who had dreamed of the temple and the monogram of Briant's name. And he knew that the hand of God was in the event of the boy's death. While this Elder spoke, his face shone with the Spirit of God, and his words thrilled every heart. Out of the hundreds who were present, probably there were no Saints who did not see a direct manifestation of the Holy Ghost on this occasion. The Elder renewed the promise which he had made to Briant during the child's lifetime; and he did it, unquestionably, by the inspiration of the Almighty. He said:

"It seems strange to our natural senses that this child shou'd be lying here, stilled in death, and yet we shou'd entertain a belief—nay, a knowledge, that he will be with the Saints in his own dear person, at the building of the temple in Jackson County. And yet, my brethren and sisters, I know that the promise made to him will be fulfilled. We are drawing nearer to that great day when wondrous things shall be manifested unto us; the veil between us and the eternal abode of our Almighty Father is growing thinner day by day. It is a'most ready to burst."

Elders Rodney C. Badger and Robert F. Neslen, of Salt Lake, also addressed the congregation. Elder Neslen, in referring to the missionary work performed by Briant Stevens, turned to a number of old veterans of the Church who were sitting upon the stand, and said:

"This dear little boy by his own efforts brought four souls into a belief in the everlasting gospel. His converts are here to day, sincere believers, full of promise and devotion to the work, and now I doubt whether some of the rest of us whose forms are bowed, and whose hair is gray, with all our wander-

ings up and down the face of the earth, can truly say that we
have done more than he."

: The little form of Briant Stevens was laid away in the ceme-
tery; but his work did not end with the vanishing of his form
from its daily associations. Of him truly it may be said that
his work lives after him. Some of his former companions
have been changed from the hour that they learned of his
death; and if there be any prospect in human life which can
be deemed certain of fulfillment, these children will be his imitators in all that was good. Word has come to his parents,
even from distant points, that children who knew him have
said since his death, "we will try to live like little Briant Stevens, so that if we should die we can be remembered."

And two of his daily associates—one of them being Fred J.
Bluth, was with him on each occasion when he broke his arm,
and the other being Edgar Peterson, one of Briant's converts,
have received a power and manifestation concerning him which
is not unworthy of mention.

Briant and Fred attended the Central School together; and
each night Briant, who was the earlier released from his classes,
waited at the gate for Fred. In the second night after Briant
was buried, Fred had a dream which he relates almost exactly
in the following words:

"I thought that Briant was waiting for me at the gate as
usual—only he was dressed in white raiment, like that in
which he lay in the coffin. When I came near him, he sprang to
my side and threw his arms around my neck. He took my
hand, and said: 'Come, Fred, with me.'

"Hand in hand, we ran up town together. We came to a
house in which a baby lay dead. We entered the room and
looked at the little one. Still hand in hand, we came out, and
a large wagon stood before the door. The driver came down
from his seat, and we got in and drove to a building like a
granary. Briant opened the doors. And then I heard a voice
saying:

" 'You must fill the wagon with corn.'

Briant and I began to shovel corn into the wagon; but soon
he stopped. I asked:

" 'Is it enough?'

"And he answered:

" 'Not yet.'

"I worked a little longer, and again I called to him:

. " 'Is it enough, Briant?'

"And once more he replied:

" 'Not yet, Fred.'

"After a still longer time, during which I worked diligently, I asked him for the third time:

" 'Is it enough?'

"And Briant replied:

" 'Yes, it is enough. Now you must come with me, Fred.'

"I climbed into the wagon with him; and then we drove away together. At once I awoke."

Little Fred felt startled by this dream. He related it to Edgar Peterson, when the latter asked:

"Do you know the meaning of your dream?"

"No."

"Then I will give you the interpretation. It means that your earthly work is not yet finished and that when it is done, Briant will call for you."

———

My young brethren and sisters, doubtless you all have ambitious moments in which you sigh to be noble, and to do some heroic action. Think of little Briant Stevens. He learned the secret of true greatness. He lived in purity, in faith and in prayer to Almighty God.

FINDING COMFORT.

The Experience of a Young Missionary in a Lonely Field, 10,000 Miles from Home.

BY THOMAS A. SHREEVE.

CHAPTER I.

CALLED TO AUSTRALASIA—THE MODERN IMITATORS OF
JOB'S FRIENDS—OUR "SPECIAL INSTRUCTION" IS TO
"BUILD UP THE KINGDOM OF GOD IN THOSE LANDS"
—A DISAPPOINTMENT ENDS IN A BLESSING—PROMISES
BY AN APOSTLE WHICH WERE LITERALLY FULFILLED
—WE REACH SYDNEY, AND I AM SEPARATED FROM
MY COMPANION.

IF a relaton of my missionary experience can give to my
young brethren and sisters one tithe of the strength and blessing which that experience itself imparted to me, I shall be
more than repaid in relating it. From the reading of similar
accounts by other Elders I have derived much benefit myself;
but I realize that words are powerless to convey a full description of the events which befall every missionary of the Church
of Jesus Christ of Latter-day Saints. No man can serve his
Savior faithfully in distant lands, among strangers, without
receiving and keeping constantly the Spirit of holiness, and

without experiencing miraculous interpositions in his behalf.
At the time of their occurrence they are subjects of wonder and
thankfulness; but as years pass by, it becomes extreme'y difficult to put them into words so expressive that they do not
seem either too fanciful for reality, or too cold to be interesting.

At the General Conference on April 8th, 1878, in company
with Elder Fred. J. May, of Salt Lake, I was called to fill a
mission in Australasia, comprising Australia, Tasmania and
New Zealand. A strange circumstance attended this calling.
For a week previous to the time that the public announcement
was made, some of the authorities who had the matter in
charge, and who had my name with the names of other missionaries, had been looking vainly for me, or for someone who
knew me. Three separate times my name was called in public
meeting, and a request for my attendance at the President's
office was made known. I heard nothing of the matter,
although probably scores of my friends and intimate acquaintances were present. But each one thought that I had either
heard the notice myself, or would be told by someone else.
At last, on Saturday evening, April 6th, 1878, I was informed
that a meeting was to be held at the Council House, and that
my presence was desired. I was then engaged in the old "Big
Boot" shoe store in Salt Lake; and I dropped my work and
hastened to the appointment, reaching the Council House just
at the appointed hour. I found Brother John Van Cott there,
and asked him what was wanted of me.

"Wanted of you?" he asked, in surprise.

"Yes, I was told that inquiry had been made for me in two
or three meetings, and that I was wanted here to-night."

"Oh, are you the man? We have been hunting for
you for a week. I have known you for years, but I had forgotten entirely who you were. We want to know if you are
willing to take a mission. Are you?"

"Yes, sir."

At that moment Uncle Joseph Young came in; and Brother
Van Cott turned to him and said:

"Uncle Joseph, here's the man we've been looking for so long."

After President Joseph had looked at me for a moment, he said: "Young man, we want to know if you are willing to take a mission. If you have any excuses to make, though, you may take them to the President's office."

I replied, "Brother Young, I have no excuses to make. I will endeavor to go whenever I am wanted."

I have since been led to marvel, and to thank my Heavenly Father, that the authorities did not drop my name from the list of missionaries at that time, instead of persisting in the search for me. No doubt it has shaped my life, and given me a blessing which will endure beyond this mortality.

I could not be present in the Tabernacle on the following Monday when the call was made, and therefore did not know to what mission I was assigned, until some over-zealous friends rushed into the place where I was employed, and informed me that I was called to Australasia, and offered me their sympathy.

During the remainder of the week I was the recipient of innumerable condolences. One brother said to me:

"That is the hardest mission in the world. No Elders are there now, and some of the men who were last called to labor in that field—educated and experienced preachers—returned in ten months utterly discouraged, and reported that no satisfactory result could be accomplished in that region."

Another brother said:

"I would rather be called to go into Montana and preach to the miners."

Another said:

"As good a Mormon as I am, I would rather go to Purgatory and preach to the spirits in prison there than to take your mission, Thomas."

And finally another one (who has since suffered martyrdom in the penitentiary)—a prominent business man of Salt Lake, by the way—said:

"The kind of missionary needed in that land is a man like Orson Pratt;" implying very strongly that inexperienced persons like myself might better stay at home than to make a use-less attempt to convert the cold and skeptical people in Aus-tralia and New Zealand to a knowledge of the gospel.

While I had made up my mind to endeavor, by the help of the Lord, to perform my duty; remarks of this kind could not help but make me despondent. I had been very much sur-prised, and somewhat shocked, I will confess, when the announcement was made to me of the nature of my mission; and these injudicious condolences intensified my self-distrust, and made me feel as if my trip would be anything but pleas-ant to myself and advantageous to the cause. But happily all my friends were not of this class. After a few days, and when I was beginning to feel considerably cast down, Elder John Van Cott met me, and said:

"Thomas, I hear that you have been having some of Job's friends to comfort you. Never mind, my boy; go and fill your mission, and you will be blessed in your labor. When I was called to go to Scandinavia I and others felt that it would be a hard mission for me—if not a useless one. But the Lord has wrought it into a ble sing for me; because I can travel through the length and breadth of this Territory, and in every settle-ment I can find a friend."

Within a week after the time we were called, Brother May and myself went to the Council House to be set apart for our labor. Fifty-two Elders, I think, were there the same day to obtain their blessing. We were among the last. In fact all the others had received their ordination and had gone before any attention was paid to us. Apostles Charles C. Rich, Orson Pratt and Lorenzo Snow were there attending to this labor: and when the last of the other missionaries had departed, Brother Rich turned to me and said:

"Well, Thomas, you are going to quit selling shoes, and going to preach the gospel, are you?"

I answered, "Yes, sir; I shall try."

They enquired unto what mission we were called; and learn-ing that we were going to distant and abandoned Australasia, they all expressed great interest in our welfare, and they sat down with us and talked very kindly for some little time.

I had watched the blessings of the other missionaries, and had noticed that the Apostles each took his turn in ordaining the young Elders to their calling. I was acquainted with Apostles Rich and Pratt, but not with Apostle Snow; and I earnestly desired that one of the two former should bless me. So I had located myself in the position where I thought Brother Rich would reach me in his turn. However, their visit with us had disarranged their plan; and when the conversation was ended one of them enquired:

"Whose turn is it to ordain this Elder?"

The result was that Brother Snow was called upon to ordain me. At the moment I was disappointed; for I realized how grave a responsibility I was going forth to meet, and I fancied I could gain greater strength and blessing under the hands of one of the Apostles with whom I had been acquainted for years, than under the hands of a stranger. But the result banished that disappointment. Brother Snow sensed our peculiar situation, and he blessed me with a power and spirit which thrilled my whole being. Before he had concluded his words the tears were coursing down my checks like rain. As if the words were uttered yesterday, I remember some promises which he made to me:

"From the moment that you leave these valleys until you return, the angels of the Almighty shall be with you. When you travel by land or by sea, though dangers may beset you on the right hand and on the left, the power of the Almighty shall protect you. Though death may stare you in the face, the angels of the Lord will warn you and shield you. Though the enemies of the truth may plot against you, their evil designs shall be made known to you by the angels of the Lord, and if you heed their warning you shall be protected. When even your brethren shall desert you and turn against you, and your way shall seem to be hedged up, you will find a blessing given you from the Lord, for He will be your friend. And you will see the day when you will have no friend with the power to aid you, other than your Heavenly Father, in all the land where you are sojourning. But we promise you that because of your faith you shall be brought triumphant through these tribulations, and shall be brought to your home again in safety and with the approbation of the Priesthood and the blessing of the Almighty. And you shall live to see the day when your labors in that far-off land will bear good fruit."

Every word of that prophetic blessing has been fulfilled in a most wonderful manner. I believe that the Lord put these things into Brother Snow's mind, and that He gave me these promises to comfort and sustain me; and that in the little disappointment which I felt at not receiving my blessing under the hands of Apostle Rich or Apostle Pratt, the Lord had really His own wise purpose to accomplish.

A week previous to the date fixed for our departure we were at President Taylor's office to learn if he had any special instruction for us. We hoped and expected that he would outline our work or that we might have some particular rule of guidance in that distant and lonely land. But the President's only word was:

"Yes, brethren, we want you to go to Australasia, and build up the Kingdom of God there."

Three times we asked our question:

"Are there any special instructions for us?"

And three times we received the answer in the President's well-known impressive manner:

"Yes, brethren, we want you to go to Australasia, and build up the Kingdom of God there."

Elder May looked at him with amazement in his eyes; and certainly if my face indicated my feeling, it betrayed the utmost surprise.

Was this all? President Taylor was the Prophet of God on earth; and we were inexperienced Elders going to a land nearly ten thousand miles away from home, to labor in a mission which had been abandoned by older and more learned men than we were. Naturally, we expected to hear what we must do when we reached Australia; how we must live; how approach the people; and how apportion our time to the various districts of that vast field.

And yet our interview was ended. President Taylor's manner and words—though very kind, and even fatherly, were

decisive; and we withdrew in some disappointment. When
we got out on the street we looked at each other in a most
woe begone manner. I do not know when I felt more forlorn
or helpless than at that hour.

But we lived and learned to bless that significant sentence,
which President Taylor uttered in his wisdom, and by the
inspiration of the Spirit. It became to us better, far better,
than a book full of the "special instructions" which we had
coveted. Whenever we were discouraged, or torn by doubt,
or oppressed by fear; we had our guide:

"Build up the Kingdom of God in those lands!"

And prayer to God invariably showed us the right means to
reach that result. If we had been dependent upon a certain
method of gospel presentation, and less dependent upon our
Heavenly Father, I am sure that we would not have been so
greatly blessed as we were in our labors.

We left Zion on Tuesday, May 7th, 1878; and sailed from
San Francisco on Monday, May 13th, 1878, on the steamer,
City of Sydney. We took steerage passage, and found ourselves in a motley crowd. There were about fifty white passengers and one hundred and twenty-five Chinamen in this part
of the ship, and we had a perfect Babel. The Chinamen
kept up their own interminable chattering. And among the
whites were Welshmen, Irishmen, Scotchmen, Jew, Gentile,
Infidel: representatives of every race and of every sect. We
even had a dynamiter on board—a person who claimed friendship with the notorious O'Donovan Rossa of New York.

The first port we made was Honolulu; where we met Elder
Henry P. Richards, of Salt Lake, and Elder Woodbury, of St.
George. They took us to the houses of the Saints, and we
had a dinner of *poi* and salt fish, "luxuries" which I tried my
best to appreciate.

On Sunday, June 2nd, we passed Sunday Island, in the
South Pacific. That night we retired to rest about ten o'clock.
After eight hours sleep we arose—and found that it was Tuesday morning at six o'clock. We had sailed across the line which
marks the beginning of the day, and had lost our twenty-four
hours. I greatly regretted this loss of Monday, and never

felt entirely reconciled to it during the two years that I was away. Fortunately for my peace of mind, on our return we made two Fridays on the same spot; and I allowed my gain of Friday to cancel my loss of Monday.

We entered Auckland harbor on Wednesday, June 5th; and sailed into Sydney Bay at half past two o'clock on Wednesday morning a week later.

We remained in the lower bay during quarantine examination; and later in the morning the *City of Sidney* steamed up to the central quay, arriving at her birth about eleven o'clock. Several hundred people were on the shore awaiting the arrival of the steamer. They were all complete strangers to me, and I did not expect anyone to meet us. But I saw in the crowd one man whom I instantly knew to be a member of the Church. I turned to point him out to Brother May, but found my companion absent. However, I watched this man attentively, feeling certain that he had come to find us, and that he was one of our brethren. The event proved my supposition to be correct. When he came on board the vessel he asked the steward for two passengers by the name of May and Shreeve. As soon as he spoke I stepped up to him and told him that I was one of the persons wanted. We shook hands; and I found him to be Brother J. Nichols.

We went to his house in Sydney, and were very kindly received. During the next several days we were engaged in a reorganization of the branch, which had become somewhat demoralized by neglect and by inattention of members.

On the 16th day of July, Elder May went to Melbourne; and we did not meet again for more than two years. It was not in our original plan to be separated for so long a time; but subsequent circumstances made that lengthy separation apparently necessary. When we looked over the field after reorganizing the Sydney Branch we discovered that it was entirely too large for us to cover within a reasonable time, if we remained together; and, though we disliked to part company, we felt that by taking separate fields we could cover twice as much ground in a given length of time as by both traveling together. We therefore arranged that Brother May should go down to

Melbourne, where he had some relatives, and thence to Tasmania; while I should remain in New South Wales until the following December. About the close of the year we should both go to New Zealand and together visit the branch of the Church there, and endeavor to enlarge the work in that locality. But this p'an, for good reasons, was never consummated entirely; and I was parted from the companion whom I had learned to love, and who was the only close friend that I could hope to have on earth in that Hemisphere—from the time of his departure from Sydney until the hour when I set foot on the steamer's deck to return home.

---•••---

CHAPTER II.

LABOR WHICH BROUGHT LITTLE COMPENSATION—A MYSTERIOUS CALL TO NEW ZEALAND—ATTACKED BY AN EVIL SPIRIT—THE VISITATION THRICE REPEATED—MEETING THE BROTHER OF A FRIEND—ON BOARD THE "WAKATIPU," BOUND FOR NEW ZEALAND.

I FELT very lonely after Brother May's departure. The next day, feeling extremely despondent, I walked out to Bondi, a point overlooking the great ocean. There I knelt down among the rocks and prayed most fervently to the Lord for comfort and help through all my trials. I derived such consolation from the communion with my Heavenly Father that I have ever since felt anxious to advise my younger brethren who go on missions, to frequently seek retired spots and there offer devotion to God and supplication for His blessing.

I then engaged in the work of visiting in Sydney and its suburbs; and succeeded in finding several persons who had once been members of the Church. It was our hope to reunite these persons with the Church and get them to renew their covenants and prepare sometime for emigration to Zion; but the majority of them were hardened. The people of New South Wales had no desire to hear or obey the gospel. Many of those who had once had membership in the Church had become Josephites, and these and all the others felt that they needed no rebaptism at our hands, for they were quite good enough without.

Although I labored willingly, and even anxiously, in this region, I never felt peaceful and contented in the city of Sydney. The very hour that I landed there, I felt a weight upon my shoulders as if something were pressing me to the earth. I was as conscious of that weight as if it had really been something physically tangible; and even when I was at the house of Brother Nichols, where we received very kind treatment, I could not rid myself of this sensation. It was only when I could get away from the city itself that I could feel at all light-hearted. I often wondered why I felt so ill at ease in Sydney, and why I could not gain greater contentment when visiting with the family of Brother Nichols there; but this matter was later solved to my understanding, if not to my satisfaction.

Not long after I was left alone I had a strange dream concerning my labors. I thought that I was called to take a mission to the East. The idea was very vivid in my mind, though no steps or time seemed to have been made clear to me. When I awoke, I thought upon the matter, and interpreted it as meaning that, after my return to Zion, I should have another mission—probably to Europe. With this view I attempted to dismiss the matter from my mind; but I found the effort futile. The idea remained persistently with me for three or four days; and then one afternoon when I took up a book and sought to read, suddenly the printed lines were blurred from me, and these words started out from the page:

"You must go to New Zealand."

I rubbed my eyes, astonished, and looked again. The words had disappeared, and for a few moments I was able to read the book. But again these words came upon the page, shutting out the printed lines from my sight:

"You are wanted in New Zealand."

This strange thing was repeated again and again. But I did not permit myself to accept it as a requirement; because I remembered the definite understanding which I had made with Brother May concerning my labors in New South Wales, and the date of our mutual journey to New Zealand in December or January following. I dropped the book for a time, and then picked it up again. The strange appearance of this command was repeated. Not only on this day and with this book did I experience this wondrous manifestation; but day after day with any book or newspaper which I attempted to read, was the appearance repeated. Not understanding that this was a command to me which I ought to obey; and feeling in a measure bound by my agreement with my companion, I could not, despite all these repeated instructions, bring myself to a compliance with it. But soon the warning took another and a stronger form, and hastened my departure, while explaining to me the strange weight which I had felt upon me in Sydney.

One day I went to Ashfield, one of the environs of Sydney, to visit Brother William Armstrong, who resided there with his family. I returned in the afternoon, feeling somewhat weary, and lay down upon a lounge in the front room of Brother Nichols' house. His wife was gossiping with a neighbor in her jocular Irish way, and I felt somewhat amused in listening to her.

Suddenly I felt myself borne down by a strange and awful power. It weighed upon my bosom and seemed to be crushing me, while it pressed also upon my mouth and threw my head over the top of the lounge. The pressure upon my face was as distinct as if it had been made by a sinewy hand pressing a cloth tightly over my mouth and nose. In the first excitement my heart beat very rapidly, and then stopped, motionless. I struggled to release myself, even reaching out with one hand and seizing the edge of the lounge, intending to draw myself down to the floor. Every effort was unavailing, and it seemed to me that I was losing myself and must soon die, if I could not obtain relief. Then the thought came to me to pray, and I cried in my inmost soul:

"Oh, Lord! help me!"

No sooner had this petition passed in thought through my mind than I was instantly released. I sprang to my feet, trembling with fear and suffering, but I made no cry and gave no explanation to those who were present.

The sensation which I experienced at the time I was in the grasp of this power was as distinctly painful as any physical suffering I ever endured, and more intense than any ordinary physical pain can be. I wondered at it, as I had not been subject to such attacks; I even bit my finger to see if I were really awake, thinking that possibly I might be in a dream. But I found it all too real. Searching my mind for some explanation, I concluded that as I had returned to the house hungry and worried, I had possibly taken too much dinner. And with this unsatisfactory explanation I forced myself to be content for the time.

A few days later I determined to fast; and in the course of the day I went to the Botanical Gardens. Upon my return, feeling somewhat faint and tired, I again lay down upon the couch. In a few minutes the awful influence once more seized me—this time with even greater power than before. I was affrighted and helpless. In the midst of my dreadful physical pain and mental torture came the realization that I was in the grasp of an evil spirit. This sudden knowledge intensified my torture. For some seconds—it seemed to me an age, my heart stood still. I felt myself slipping away, but could not move nor cry aloud. Once more the inspiration came to me to pray, and I called upon my Heavenly Father for help. At once the influence departed, and I sprang to my feet weak and trembling. I felt every hair on my head standing upright.

I recalled the description given by Joseph Smith of the darkness which enveloped him when he first prayed in the woods for light; and I knew that I had experienced in some slight degree the same torment which he encountered on that occasion. I remembered that the Prophet spoke of giving up under the torture that he was suffering, and of his being saved by the power of God just at the moment when he felt himself slipping away into death and perdition. This, though undoubtedly in a greatly moderated degree, was my own experience.

After this the feeling that I must go to New Zealand was borne irresistibly. The last emphatic warning had shown me that Sydney was no place for me at this hour, and that I must heed the commandments which were given to me. Accordingly, I purchased a ticket for Port Littleton, distant about twelve hundred miles from Sydney.

The steamer by which I was to sail would not leave for a week, but I could not rest easy until I had secured my passage. The vessel was called the *Wakatipu*, from two Maori words, waka, meaning canoe, and tipu, meaning goods; the union signifying a canoe or ship to carry goods.

After purchasing this ticket the feeling of anxiety and unrest which had possessed me departed, and I felt quite content in the full consciousness that I was now in the line of my duty; but I still had a dread of the evil influences which I now knew abounded in Sydney and inhabited the house at which I was staying.

When now I took up a book or a newspaper I could see the words as distinctly as ever, and was no more visited by the commandment which had been so manifest on other occasions.

The couch on which I had lain when seized by these dark powers was my own bed at night, and I had not been troubled in the evening. But from the hour of the second seizure I religiously avoided sitting or reclining upon the lounge in the day-time. I had a strong horror of sleeping upon this couch at night, but I had no alternative; and solaced myself by constant prayer and humility before the Lord, asking to be protected from the assaults of the adversary.

Previous to taking my departure for New Zealand I went out to Ashfield to bid Brother Armstrong and his family farewell. Again I returned late in the evening. I thoughtlessly threw myself upon the couch, and almost in the very second I was seized by the destroyer. The experience was the same as on the other occasions, except that it was much more powerful and painful. I believed for a moment that I must die; but once more I was restored by my prayer to heaven. The sensations I suffered in these seizures I never can forget. To speak of them even at this hour causes a chill of horror to pass over my being, and as a rule I feel a dreadful pain attacking my heart.

I did not speak of these experiences to anyone in Sydney, nor to anyone else for a long time. I was inexperienced in these matters, and I thought it wise to keep my own counsel. But nearly a year afterward I received a letter from Brother May, who had returned to Sydney and had stopped at the house of Brother Nichols, while I was in New Zealand. He had occupied as a bed the couch whereon I had slept; and he informed me that he had been seized by evil spirits in the night, dragged from his bed, and tortured. After this reinforcement of my own views I wrote to Brother May, informing him of what had occurred at the house on three separate occasions when I was lying upon that couch. I felt then that not only was the city of Sydney an oppressive place for the Elders, but that the house where we had stopped, though occupied by a man who professed the faith, offered a welcome to evil influences. Such an opinion was substantiated later when Nichols and his wife turned Brother May out of the house, and then apostatized and joined the Josephites.

Although they had treated me very kindly I always felt under a restraint when I was on their premises; and the event showed that they preferred association with the powers of darkness to the friendship and company of the Elders of the Church.

Mrs. Nichols and her eldest son are dead; and the man, if alive, leads what I imagine must be a lonely and unsatisfactory life. I am convinced that he knows the gospel to be true; for I have had proof that he possesses this knowledge. Realizing this, I imagine that his mind must be in a dreadful state of remorse and anxiety;

The day before I was to take the steamer *Wakatipu* I went to the post office at Sydney to mail some letters. While standing at the stamp window a man walked quickly up through the crowd, thrust a paper under my face into the window, and cried:

"Foreign stamp—quick, please!"

He laid the paper down, and I saw the address upon it. To my amazement it was:

"JOHN ALFORD,
    Salt Lake City, Utah Territory, U. S. A."

I looked at the gentleman and said:—

"I beg pardon, sir; but do you know the gentleman to whom you are sending this paper?"

"Yes, sir. My brother, sir. Do you know him?"

"Yes, sir."

"Meet me here at twelve o'clock."

And with these words he was gone like a flash.

It was then eleven o'clock and I had an hour to wait. I strolled around for a short time, and promptly at twelve o'clock I was on the veranda of the post office, awaiting the coming of the very abrupt gentleman. On the stroke of the hour he dodged between the pillars of the veranda, rushed through the crowd, and beckoned me to him. Then he started at a rapid rate down the street, and I followed. After going a short distance he turned and asked me:

"Had your dinner?"

"No, sir."

"Come along, then."

We entered the Free Mason Hotel, the dining room of which was crowded. Seating ourselves at a table he gave his order for a beefsteak; and I was too good a Britisher to refuse the same.

While we were waiting, he asked if I were acquainted with his brother. I answered that I was, having worked for the same institution which employed him, for a number of years.

At his request I gave him such information as I possessed about Brother John Alford and his family, and by this time the steaks were ready, and he proceeded to eat his hurriedly.

I saw there was no time for talking, unless I wished to lose my dinner, so I plied knife and fork vigorously. When we were through he paid the charge, and we walked out.

Then he asked how long I had been in Australia. I answered:

"About two months."

"How long shall you stay?"

"Until to-morrow at one o'clock, when I leave for New Zealand by the steamer *Wakatipu.*"

"Are you a Mormon Elder?"

"Yes, sir."

"Do you travel like my brother did when he was preaching in England what you folks call the gospel—without purse or scrip?"

"Yes, sir."

"It is a very strange faith you people have. He never did any work while he was in England preaching, but he could go anywhere he wanted to go—while I, who was always working, never had either time or money to go anywhere. Curious, isn't it?"

"Yes, sir—our faith is a strange one to the world. But we are placed in such a position that we have learned to rely upon God, our Eternal Father, whose gospel we are preaching. We know that while we are executing His commands, He will provide the means."

Mr. Alford shook his head incredulously, and muttered:

"Queer faith—strange faith—I can't see it. I am busy now. Come to-morrow at twelve o'clock. I will meet you at the post office. I want to see you."

I replied:

"I must leave at one o'clock. I will scarcely have time to meet you."

"Nonsense! Come. That steamer won't sail before four or five o'clock."

Promptly at the appointed time the next day I was at the post office, and again met Mr. Alford. He shook me warmly by the hand and said:

"I expect, young man, you haven't got very much money."

"You are right," I answered.

In purchasing my ticket to Littleton I had expended my last shilling. My destination was the town of Rangiora, some distance from Port Littleton, and I needed means to pay my fare to that place.

Mr. Alford pressed ten shillings in my hand, at the same time saying:

"I do not understand how you folks can travel without purse or scrip."

I could have explained to him how his ten shillings had relieved me, and enabled me to fulfill the commands of my Master; but I saw that he was a business man—skeptical and unapproachable to the message which I was bearing to the world, and I made no attempt to encroach further upon his time.

I went on board the vessel during the afternoon, and felt that I was obeying the sacred behest which had been so often and so mysteriously repeated to me in Sydney. But the adversary seemed determined to cling to me and to fill my mind with evil thoughts. I tried to banish sadness by gazing from the deck of the moving vessel at the beautiful city of Sydney and the still more beautiful bay. But the effort was vain; my prevailing emotion was one of despondency. The ship, the receding lands, the sea into which we were passing—all seemed so vast; and I seemed such a lonely mite, that I could not find comfort in that hour.

Gradually, as the night came on, the shores grew indistinct. Only a myriad of lights twinkled out to show where the city lay. From vessels riding at anchor or moving up the bay to moor after their long voyages, came shouts of masters and songs of men. The azure depths of sky and sea held each its countless stars. But the beauty of the scene only made me more impressionable to melancholy; and I took one long farewell look at the light-dotted city and the light-dotted bay—lovely beyond description—and then went below.

I have never seen Sydney since that lonely hour.

CHAPTER IV.

An Irreverent Company of Passengers—Sickness and
    a Horror of Life Fall Upon Me—A "Helpful
    Vision"—"Only be True"—Invoking the Name of
    Christ—A Jolly Singer and a Jolly Song—Land-
    ing at Port Littleton—Strange Recognition of
    Brother Nordstrand—His Dream Concerning Me.

ON board the *Wakatipu* was a large company of worldly
    people, representing nearly all professions and stations in
life. The majority of the people were extremely sociable, and
very soon after we got out into the open water a number of
passengers gathered in the cabin with musical instruments, to
while away an hour and to banish sadness. They made a great
medley of their pleasures; and some of them were decidedly
irreverent. A portion of the party wished to dance, and the
man who supplied the music claimed to know but one tune.
This was:

"Sweeping through the gates of the New Jerusalem,
    Washed in the blood of the Lamb."

And to this very strange "schottische" some of them
danced a merry-go-round.

Notwithstanding the gaiety on board, the feeling of dread
grew upon me. It seemed to possess my very soul. Probably
I had given way too much to sadness in gazing upon the distant lights of Sydney, and now I could not banish the evil
thoughts which thronged my mind.

All manner of gloomy forebodings oppressed me. While
I remained in Sydney, I felt that there was some tie between
myself and my companion; but now I felt that I had cut
myself adrift even from him.

This was the first time in my life that ever I felt how completely alone a man can be when surrounded by joyous company. I tried to think of comfort and companionship at the end of my voyage; but the reflection proved to be an unfortunate one, because I knew no soul in all New Zealand. Death must actually be something to dread for any person to whom it will bring the appalling loneliness which possessed me at this hour.

I retired to my berth, as you may imagine, in no pleasant frame of mind. The next morning, Friday, I awoke and found myself in a raging fever. I was not sea-sick, and, though I am subject to this trouble, during this entire voyage I felt no touch of it. The fever increased during the day, until it seemed as if my whole body. were being consumed in a furnace.

No one came to enquire for me, or to offer aid; for I was not only a total stranger, but a steerage passenger—two things which, united, shut me out from help or sympathy. On Saturday morning I was worse. My tongue was swollen until it filled my mouth; it was as dry as a piece of tinder. With the intense heat of my body my teeth crumbled at a touch.

On Sunday morning I was worse; though probably the fever had not increased in intensity, because it could not; but I was very much weaker. That afternoon a passenger came to the berth, and offered me a glass of water. I took it gratefully; and this was the sole attention I received during four days.

Naturally I felt dispirited. I had not even the advantage of delirium, which accompanies most serious fevers; I was constantly awake to the full appreciation of the torture which my mind and body were enduring. Tempted by the destroyer, I felt that death would have been a welcome release from my pain. The horror was almost unbearable.

On Sunday night, the entire company of passengers, with the exception of myself, gathered in the main cabin, upon invitation of a jolly doctor, who held what he called:

"A Saturday Night at Sea."

To every person who could sing or make a speech, some part was assigned for the general amusement. From my berth in the steerage—by drawing away the curtains, I could look out upon the festive scene, in which I could bear no part, for I was helpless and speechless.

The doctor had been a surgeon in the hospitals of England, and also in the Crimean War, and he opened the entertainment by a lecture upon the strange experiences of a British army surgeon and hospital physician. While he was talking upon this suggestive subject, my mind was led to a contemplation of death. I felt with a kind of listlessness that I would soon be beyond the reach of earthly physicians, unless something could speedily be done for my relief.

After a severe struggle I so far overcame the dreadful feeling with which the adversary had filled my heart that I was able to call upon the Lord in prayer. As I silently communed with Him, I gained power; my faith was restored, and my hope for life was quickened.

I asked Him in the name of the Lord Jesus to be merciful unto me; I felt then at perfect liberty to speak to Him as a son would talk with a good earthly father. I said that I had come into this distant region—not to fulfil my own worldly wish, but at the behest of His servants, to proclaim His gospel, and to build up His Kingdom. My companion was hundreds of miles distant from me, and I was beyond the reach of earthly help or earthly sympathy. It was my earnest desire to be restored to life, that I might fulfil the mission to which I had been assigned by His representatives on earth; and to this end I asked that some aid might be given me to rebuke the devil, and to banish the horrors which I felt would soon, if allowed to work their way, bring dissolution.

When my prayer was ended, I heard the doctor still talking; but under the sound of his voice I fell asleep.

I dreamed that I was back in Sydney, sick in bed. Brother May was at a table in the room, and we were conversing. Across the room, to the right of my bed, was an open door, which I could see without lifting my head from the pillow.

While I lay there listening to the words of Brother May, a personage clothed in a white robe entered the room. He appeared to be a young man, and had a very pleasing countenance. This personage passed around the bed and stood near the table. Brother May rose and offered the visitant a chair, and then withdrew. The young man seated himself at the table and opened a book. He said:

"Are you ready to report the Sydney Branch?"

"Yes, sir," I responded.

"Then proceed."

I gave him an account of all our doings in Sydney, begining with our first effort of reorganizing, and closing with my last act previous to sailing—for all these things seemed plain to my mind. The recital seemed to occupy me several minutes, and I continued to speak freely. He wrote in the book rapidly, and never once interrupted me. I felt that he was taking every word I uttered. When I stopped, he asked:

"Have you anything more to say?"

"No, sir," I answered.

Then he turned the leaves back, and seemed to read from the beginning. He said:

"Very well. Now where are you going?"

"To New Zealand."

He recorded my answer in the book, and then signed his name—I could not see the words of his name, but I felt that he was writing his own signature. He closed the book and walked around to the right side of the bed, shook hands with me, and said:

"Good-by; I will be there before you."

He passed from the room, and then I saw the figure of a little child standing at the foot of the bed. I looked closely and recognized my little brother Teddy, who had been drowned nearly twenty years before. I seemed to know that he had come from the spirit world, and in my anxiety I sprang from the bed, and, resting one knee upon the floor, I gazed intently at him. He stepped near me, and I took one little arm in my hand. Although a spirit, he seemed palpable to my touch. I said:

"I think you are my little brother Teddy; but it is so long since I saw you that I had almost forgotten how you looked."

Then the thought came into my mind that I must ask him some question. I said:

"Teddy, have you seen our Heavenly Father yet?"

He answered in the sweet voice of a child:

"No—but I shall see Him."

I noticed that he was trembling, and that from his eyes there went a glance of fear to the open door. I asked again:

"Have you brought any message to me?"

To this question he answered, "Yes," shaking at the time more violently with fear; but he turned his glance from the door and his eyes looked straight into mine, and he came nestling into my arms. He lifted the fore finger of his right hand toward my face and said:

"Only be true!"

He turned his head, still with that frightened glance, at the open door, and this time I also looked. And I saw an evil spirit standing just outside and shaking its fist at the little one, and bearing on its face a demoniacal scowl. Its whole bearing and gesture implied the words, "Don't you dare to give that message!"

When I saw this, I said to Teddy:

"Have no fear—I know how to drive him away."

For even in my dream I seemed to understand what power the evil one possessed and how he could be rebuked. And I seemed now to have got back my faith and the power of my calling. I strode to the door and stood close to the wicked spirit. I raised my arm to the square, with my hand open and the palm extended toward him, saying at the same time:

"In the name of the Lord Jesus Christ of Nazareth, the Son of the living God, I command you to be gone."

He looked at me with a hateful glare, but slowly walked three or four steps down the stairway which was there. Then he stopped, folded his arms, and, looking at me defiantly, cried:

"I will not go! I will not go! I will not go!"

I said:

"You will go."

And then I followed him down, again standing close to him.
Again I brought my arm to the square and repeated my solemn
adjuration. He walked down the stairs and took refuge in a
corner. This time he assumed a most resolute mein. His
face expressed intense malice and hatred. He cried:

"I will not go—you shall not drive me away!"

For the last time I invoked that supreme name of our Lord
Jesus, and then the demon—shaking his hands at me still in
a threatening manner, fled with a look of baffled rage on his
hideous countenance.

I returned to the room and found that Teddy was gone.

Weak and exhausted I climbed back into my bed and
seemed to fall asleep; and at the very instant when I seemed
to lapse into slumber I awoke with a start and heard the sound
of a jolly song.

Instead of the dry parched feeling which had enveloped my
whole being when I fell asleep, I was now in a delicious per-
spiration. From my face the sweat was rolling in little streams.
This seemed as pleasant to me as a flood of water to a thirsty
desert.

The singing came from the cabin. The man who was giving
the song in a full, manly voice, was so near to my berth that I
could have reached out and placed my hand upon his shoulder.
The chorus of his song went to my heart; and I afterward
learned that the young man had not been invited to sing, but
had been seized with a sudden impulse, unaccountable even to
himself. To this hour I have treasured in my recollection the
comforting words of that chorus. They were:

> "Never, boys, give way to sorrow,
>   But be up and act like men!
> Look with hope for joys to-morrow—
>   Sunny days shall come again!"

When again I fell asleep I was comparatively happy. The
following morning when I awoke I was well, except for great
weakness.

Many hours subsequently, while I lay wide-awake and comfortable in my berth—lulled by the swirl of waters against the
ship—I saw, standing on a step-ladder by the side of my berth

and looking down upon me, a little old lady. She was short and stout, and pleasant-looking. Her eyes gleamed with kindness, and she smiled in a most friendly fashion. How she came there 1 knew not, but she seemed to feel perfectly at home.

When my eyes met hers, she began to nod at me. She continued her droll recognition for several moments, and then she spoke in a jolly tone:

"I know you; I know you! And you shall know me when we meet again."

Then she disappeared as suddenly as she had come. But her face and figure, her smile and twinkling eyes, and her good-natured voice remained long with me as a pleasant memory. Before I had been a very long time in New Zealand, I saw her again; but this next time her presence was more than a fleeting fancy.

At ten o'clock on Tuesday morning we sighted New Zealand. At eight o'clock that night we arrived at the port of Wellington. It was in the ordinary time of the steamer that we should leave at four o'clock the next morning on the voyage across Cook's Strait to Littleton, my destination—175 miles distant.

Instead, however, of our getting away Wednesday morning at four o'clock, at that hour a furious gale was coming up the strait. So terrific was its power that the captain could not entertain the thought of going out of port; so we remained over twenty-six hours, and left Wellington at six o'clock on Thursday morning.

On Friday morning, about six o'clock, we reached Port Littleton, from which place I had learned that a train started for Christchurch, on the way to Rangiora, an hour later. It was my intention to go on shore with my luggage and take a seat in this train before seven o'clock.

But, as I was about to set foot upon the gangway, I felt a sudden prompting, as distinct as if it were a voice, speaking to me:

"Don't go ashore now. You must wait for a time."

I learned that another train would leave during the morning, and then I went back into the cabin with my luggage and remained nearly an hour. While waiting I seemed to hear a voice as of someone speaking behind me:

"Now is your time to go ashore."

I took all my luggage on my shoulders and in my hands, and walked across the deck and gangway, and was just setting foot on the quay, when a man rushed up to me and said:

"Excuse me, sir; but do you know of anyone by the name of Shreeve on board this vessel?"

I dropped my luggage, reached out my hand, and said:

"You are Brother Nordstrand!"

He replied:

"Yes; and you are Brother Shreeve! Allow me to welcome you to New Zealand."

I did not know at the time why I said "Brother Nordstrand." Of course I had never seen the man before, and the only possible acquaiutance I could have had with his name, was, that I·had glanced once or twice, some weeks previous, at a report which contained the names of the New Zealand Saints. Paying but little attention to this matter at the time, I did not remember that Nordstrand was among these names, even if I saw it. I had no idea that any person would come to meet me. And yet I spoke his name and reached out my hand to him with as much confidence as if we had been old acquaintances, only separated for a year or two.

If this experience on my own part seemed marvelous to me, upon reflection, I was still more surprised when Brother Nordstrand related the events which caused him to meet the *Wakatipu* at Port Littleton. He said:

"I live at Styx. This morning in a dream, a personage—a young man of pleasing appearance, clothed in a white robe—visited me and instructed me to go to Port Littleton this morning and meet the steamer *Wakatipu*, and find among her passengers a man named Shreeve, who was a "Mormon" Elder coming to visit the Saints in New Zealand. The vision was so vivid that I was roused from my sleep; and, when it was ended, I sprang out of bed and looked at the clock. I found the hour to be four A. M. Two hours later I saddled my horse and rode to Christchurch, a distance of six or seven miles. There I took train for Port Littleton, nine miles away, and arrived here to meet you."

The sole information and instruction upon which Brother Nordstrand acted was that conveyed to him in this dream. In a later conversation I learned that in the same vision he had been shown all the consequences which would attend upon my ministration in New Zealand. The event proved that this dream to Brother Nordstrand was one of the greatest blessings of my life. I encountered much tribulation in New Zealand; no more from the bigotry of the world than from the perfidy of my own brethren. But through all the trouble Brother Nordstrand was my devoted friend. He had never a moment of doubt, because all which happened had been by him foreseen.

CHAPTER V.

REASON FOR MY SUDDEN CALL TO LEAVE SYDNEY—THE
LITTLE OLD LADY OF THE "WAKATIPU"—SHE HAD
WAITED A GENERATION TO RENEW HER COVENANTS—
ANOTHER "HELPFUL VISION"—A MYSTERIOUS HALF-
SOVEREIGN—SAVED FROM DEATH IN A SWIFT RIVER.

ELDERS William McLachlan, Thomas Steed, Charles Hurst and Fred. Hurst had been the last Utah Elders to labor in the New Zealand missionary field previous to the date of my landing there. They had rendered good service to the cause, and I discovered that the foundation which they had laid was broad and deep, and cemented in gospel truth.

After a few days visit with Brother Nordstrand at Styx, I went to Southbrook, where I found Elder James Burnett Jr., the young man who had been left in charge of the mission by the brethren about a year before.

With him and with others I labored up and down the country in that locality, and in the ensuing three months twenty-five souls were brought into the Church in the Canterbury Province.

One of my first meetings was held at Prebbleton. While speaking there, I felt led to detail the strange succession of circumstances attendant upon my coming so early to that field. When I sat down a good sister named Mortensen arose and said:

"Brother Shreeve, I can tell you why you received the command to come to New Zealand immediately. It was in answer to our fervent prayer. For more than three months previous to your arrival here we had been anxiously supplicating the Lord to send us an Elder from Utah."

About two months after I landed in New Zealand I was traveling in company with Brother John Walker, when he said to me:

"There is a woman living in this neighborhood, who, I understand, once belonged to the Church. I am acquainted with her husband. Let us go over and see her."

I assented to his proposition and went to the house designated. When we entered we saw a little old woman sitting by the stove, smoking a pipe. She arose with some embarrassment at receiving visitors. But the moment she fully confronted me, I saw that she was the little old woman who had visited me in imagination on board the *Wakatipu*, while sailing across Cook's Straits.

I learned that her name was Sister Emmas, and in conversation she stated to me that she had become a member of the Church a generation before, in the town of Bristol in England. It was there that the miracle of restoration of sight was performed under the administration of Elder John Hackwell, upon the eyes of the children of William and Elizabeth Bounsell. Sister Emmas had been an eye witness to this miracle. She was then firm in the faith; but the young man whom she married—being anxious to get her away from the influence of the hated "Mormons" had carried her to this remote nook in New Zealand, thinking that he had separated her from the Church forever.

She had often prayed to be visited by members of the Church and to be united with her people. Some years before I met her a man had worked for her husband for a brief time, and then departed. After he was gone she learned that he was a "Mormon." He had interested her greatly while he labored for her husband, and she had been unable to account for the interest she took in him. After he was gone the matter was explained to her satisfaction; and she looked anxiously for his return—but in vain, for she never saw him after that hour.

In later conversations I spoke to her of her appearance to me on board the *Wakatipu*, and by comparison of dates I learned that on or about the very day when she appeared to me, she had been praying most earnestly that the Lord would bless her with a visit from a "Mormon" Elder. She had often sat by her window and looked out with straining eyes and anxious heart for someone to come to her, and bring a renewal of the glad tidings which she had heard thirty years before in England.

While I remained in that region Sister Emmas was very kind to me. She frequently helped me with money, and I was always a welcome visitor at her house.

She loved to talk about the things of the gospel, but I found that she was but a child. She had heard nothing of the teachings of the Church except those earliest taught in England, and the sublime doctrines of baptism for the dead, and other things revealed to the Saints later than her day in the Church were entirely new and strange to her. Often when I was talking she would clasp her hands, and look at me with the utmost surprise, saying:

"Well, well! Now they didn't teach that when I joined the Church—I didn't understand it that way."

But she seemed always willing to learn, and was indeed a faithful soul. Her husband, however, continued bitterly opposed, and after some time both she and I agreed that for the sake of her peace it would be better if my visits to their house ceased. But before we finally parted the good old lady said to me:

"You will know when I am dead—I will let you know; and then, if there is anything which you can do for my eternal blessing, I pray you to do it."

On the 27th of February, 1879, I went to the North Island, in the hope to do some successful labor there. At Wellington I stopped at a hotel kept by a Mr. Davil'e, a relative of Brother C. W. Carter of Salt Lake. On the night of my arrival I retired to my room, wet and cold. I was wearied, but wakeful, because of my anxiety. I knew that several efforts had been made in times past to open the work in this region; but they seemed all to have been unsuccessful, and I doubted my own ability to accomplish any good. I felt prayerful, but still despondent.

While I lay, wide awake, in my bed I suddenly saw a hand and arm, clothed in a white sleeve which extended down midway between the elbow and the wrist, and holding a torch in its hand —thrust out from the side of a dark fireplace which was in the room.

At first there was but a spark of light at the top of the torch, but gradually the flame grew greater and the light stronger, until it filled the whole room; and then from out the darkness behind the arm and torch stepped the figure of a little girl.

I recognized it instantly as that of my young sister Sophia, who had died six years before in England, while I was in Utah. At the time of her death she was eight and a half years old, and had but recently been baptized into the Church. She came toward the bed, and I saw that she was dressed in beautiful white raiment. From her whole person a pleasing light seemed to emanate. She approached the bed and leaned over it, placing her arms around my neck and kissing me upon the lips. Then, still with her hands clasped, she leaned back and looked intently into my face, saying at the same time:

"Tom, don't be afraid! Whenever you are in danger I will come to warn you."

She bent forward and kissed me again; afterward leaning back to take another look at my face. Repeating the same words as before, once more she kissed me; and then slowly withdrew her arms and moved back from the bed. She approached the arm, which still held the torch, and as she did so I saw that the light of the torch paled before the greater glory which surrounded her person. When she neared the fireplace the arm stretched out around her, and she stepped back into the darkness. She waved her hand three times with a farewe'l gesture toward me. Soon she was enveloped in the darkness of the fireplace, and the light of the torch grew for a moment brighter; then suddenly it vanished and I found myself leaning upon my elbow in the bed and gazing fixedly at the blank darkness where the glorious presence and the light torch had disappeared. So real and certain had been the presence of my sister that after she was gone I still felt he pressure of her warm arms around my neck.

I remained in that region for a time, but could not find any opening; and therefore concluded to return to the South Island. At the time I greatly regretted the necessity for this step, for it seemed like a desertion of the field; but I was later led to thank God for the guidance of the Spirit for taking me away from the North Island.

It had been my purpose to obtain an opening among the Maories, and proclaim to them the gospel; but two weeks after my return to the South Island serious trouble broke out between the government and the Maori tribes which I had intended to visit on the west coast. This trouble continued for a considerable time, and during it, whenever my mind recurred to the subject, I thanked the Lord that I had been led away from that locality; because the people of that region would have been only too glad to attribute the Maori uprising to the "incendiary presence" of a Mormon Elder.

One day after my return, myself and a companion had been baptizing at Alfred Forest and it was our desire to reach Templeton as speedily as possible. We were very tired, having walked thirty-two miles that day, and we concluded to ride from Rakaia to Templeton, provided we had enough money for the purpose. We emptied all our pockets very carefully. I took especial care to feel in every corner of my clothing, and I gave all I had to my companion, who said that with his little stock this was barely sufficient to purchase the tickets. When we arrived at Templeton we learned that Brother Walker was quite ill at his home in a little town two or three miles distant.

When I arose to dress the next morning, I happened to put my hand in my vest pocket; and to my amazement I drew forth a half-sovereign in gold. How it came there I know not to this day: I was possessed of such a coin so infrequently in those days that I had certainly not placed it in my pocket and forgotten it; besides only the night previous at Rakaia I had searched my pockets carefully and had given every penny possessed to my fellow-laborer.

At the request of my companion, who was too weary to attempt the journey, I trudged down that morning to Brother Walker's house—although I myself had been so tired that I thought I could not walk a furlong. When I reached the house I found Brother Walker was indeed very sick; and that, owing to the confinement occasioned by his sickness, his business had been neglected, and his folks had been unable to leave him while they made collections of money due him, and they were for the moment in a very needy state, not having a penny in the house.

When I found the situation in which they were placed I said to Sister Walker:

"I have found a half-sovereign this morning, which came to me in some unknown way for some unknown purpose; and now I shall be glad to let you have it for your needs."

She thanked me, and told me that she would be grateful if I would hitch up their horse and drive over to Christchurch and purchase some bread and medicine. I did as she requested. I hitched up the horse and went immediately to Christchurch, a distance of three or four miles.

Arrived there I went to the baker's shop and asked for two shillings and sixpence worth of bread, giving the baker in payment my half-sovereign, or ten shilling piece. He gave me the proper change I am sure, because I watched it carefully. I placed this change of silver in the empty purse which I had in my hand, and then went to the chemist's shop. Here I purchased medicine to the amount of two shillings, and took that much money from the purse and paid the chemist.

Then I hastened back to Brother Walker's, and when I entered the house I gave the folks the bread and the medicine, and tossed the purse, containing as I supposed, five shillings and sixpence in change, to Sister Walker. She emptied the money into her lap, counted it, and then said:

"You did not pay for the bread and medicine which you got at Christchurch."

I replied that I had paid for them, certainly; because, being unknown to the baker and chemist, they would not have trusted me.

"But," she replied, "you have brought back ten shillings and four pence—which is more than you carried away with you."

I answered that I could not help that—I had certainly paid for the bread and the medicine and had received my exact change from the baker, who broke the money for me.

But whatever I might say, there was the money—four pence more than I had carried away, although I had spent four shillings and sixpence.

Some time afterward I was requested by Jeppe C. Jeppeson to go to Alfred Forest to perform for him and his family the ordinance of baptism. I was then at Prebbleton, and Alfred Forest was more than seventy miles away.

The second day of my journey I had thirty-two miles to travel on foot from the Rakaia River to Alfred Forest. My way lay for ten miles along the bank of the Rakaia; and thence along a level stretch for twenty miles, to the North Ashburton River. This I would be obliged to cross, and from the crossing to travel for two miles to the residence of Mr. Jeppeson. The Rakaia is a broad river flowing between high and steep banks.

The day was extremely hot, with a north-west wind blowing. This "north-wester" as it is called in that region is something like the desert simoon—it dries the sap out of everything. It is intensely hot and parching in its nature, and quickly enervates any person exposed to its influence. Especially is this the case with a person unaccustomed to the climate.

Whenever I wanted to moisten my lips I had considerable difficulty in descending to the stream and reascending the steep and high bank. But I was soon spared this annoyance; because when I began to cross the plain I found no water whatever. There was not a drop to be found for a stretch of nearly fifteen miles. Several times during this painful journey I lay down, feeling utterly exhausted; and once or twice I felt that death would be a relief.

. About a mile before I, reached the north fork of the Ashburton, I saw a stick about six feet long and two inches thick, lying across my path. I passed it by, but could not help feeling greatly surprised at seeing it there; because I had not, during the whole time that I was walking across this plain seen any tree or shrub or even a willow of any kind. After I had gone some distance, I felt an impression that I ought to turn back and get the stick. I endeavored to put this idea from my mind, but without avail; and so I returned and picked up the stick and carried it with me.

When I reached the river I expected to find someone there to meet me; because Mr. Jeppeson had promised that his son would await me on the north side of the river with a horse, and help me across. But I found no one there.

The sun had long gone down, and darkness was swiftly descending upon the earth. The river was rapidly rising for the north-wester was the warning of a storm which had been raging in the mountains. This branch of the Ashburton was about a furlong in width, and was naturally a rapid though not deep stream. Its fall was so great that an immense quantity of water could be carried with a shallow depth. As with many other New Zealand rivers, for a single person to cross on foot was a dangerous experiment, because the water flows so rapidly that one is easily lifted off his feet; and once down he could never get up again.

I was debating in my mind whether I should pass the night on the north bank of the river, or run the risk of death in crossing, when I saw a rift like a triangle open in the clouded sky to the south. From this rift sufficient light came to enable me to see the surface of the stream. I looked from the roadway and saw that at various points in the river were shifting sand bars, which I could detect by the rippling over them of the rising waters.

I knelt down and prayed for guidance from my Heavenly Father, and when I arose it was with a determination to cross the stream. I descended into the water, but some influence immediately forced me back to shore. This influence was so powerful that it lifted me back to the bank like a cork.

Then I bent over and looked at the stream, and by the aid of the light from the open space in the sky I saw that where I intended to enter the river was a deep, dark current. Higher up I could see that the light shone on a line of ripples, betokening sand bars, extending almost entirely across the stream. I ascended to a favorable point and saw that here the light shone at its brightest; and I took this line for my ford.

I had the stick which I had providentially picked up, and this I put into the water down stream from me, and grounded it on the bottom, and then I entered without fear. I leaned up stream as far as I could without falling, and, although the stream was only up to my knees, the pressure of the swift current against my body threw it as high as my waist. As soon as I could gain a firm footing upon the bottom, I moved my stick from point to point; and in this way progressed safely to the first bar. Then I stepped into a hole with my right foot, and caught myself just as I was going down.

A cold sweat broke out on me, because, while I had not had much experience with New Zealand rivers, I knew perfectly well that to lose my footing was to die. I stood a moment to breathe and to recover my composure, and then I started on.

Guided by the light, and supported by my stick, I was able to zig zag from one bar to another, until I was within twenty yards of the south bank. Then again I missed my footing, and was whirled around and nearly cast down. The stick once more saved me, and in a few minutes I was safely landed on the shore.

Wet, exhausted with the long battle in crossing the river, my shoes full of sand and my feet raw; I sank down upon the ground, wearied but joyful. I thanked God for the preservation of my life through the struggle with the fierce river.

When I rose from my knees I looked up at the sky, and saw that the providential light (which had undoubtedly been the means of saving my life) had disappeared. I felt convinced from this that there were no more streams; and the result proved the correctness of that idea.

I walked on two miles and found the house of Mr. Jeppeson; but it was closed up, all the people having retired to bed. When I found that they had preferred to retire, rather than to fulfill their engagement with me, I went to the house of Brother Olsen, who kindly gave me supper and a bed.

A few days later, Mr. Jeppeson came to me with profuse apologies, and at his request I baptized him and his family.

CHAPTER V.

SOME OLD MEMBERS OF THE CHURCH—THE SPIRIT PROMPTS PROMISES TO THEM WHICH ARE LITERALLY FULFILLED —HELP FROM A CATHOLIC WHO IS SUDDENLY CONVERTED AND WHO AS SUDDENLY APOSTATIZES—A SPONTANEOUS PROPHECY—THE JOURNEY HOME—A CAREFUL OBSERVER—SAFE IN ZION.

ONE day while visiting at a little village called Greytown, I met a lady whose name was Mrs. Reid. She had belonged to the Church fifteen or sixteen years before, when she was a girl in England. She had been quite a devoted member of the Church, and some of the Elders promised her that through her faithfulness and her kindness she should be enabled to gather to Zion with the Saints. This was the dearest wish of her heart, and she fondly anticipated the time. But she was courted by a man whom she subsequently married, and he came into the Church for the purpose of gaining her hand. The time was almost set for her departure to the Valley; but he insisted that they should be married in England. The Elders advised her to wait until she and her affianced could reach Zion; but she was persuaded by the pleadings of Mr. Reid, and married him in England. No sooner were they united than he took her to another part of the country, and later he carried her to New Zealand. He had not been sincere in his protestations of faith, but had merely joined the Church for the purpose of gaining her hand.

She had repented bitterly this error of her life, and when I saw her she was a most lonely and miserable creature. Her mother and sisters were in Utah, but she had no hope of ever seeing them. Her husband was a besotted wretch who made her life one continued agony.

She unfolded to me all the troubles of her life. She recalled clearly all that had been promised to her by the Elders, and she wept when she thought of how she had robbed this sacred promise of its fulfillment by her own lack of fidelity. She blamed no one but herself, but she said to me very sorrowfully before we parted:

"I know that my husband will not permit me to be rebaptized. He is angry because you come here; for he thinks that the "Mormons" have again hunted me out. But before you go away I want you to bless me and my children."

I complied with her request, and when my hands were on her head I felt led to promise her, in the name of the Lord, that she should be released from her trouble, and that very shortly. A few months later I learned that she was dead. I did not understand the full significance of the promise which I gave, at the time. I only spoke the words in obedience to the inspiration of the Spirit; but I am satisfied that this was the only relief which could come to this poor, oppressed woman, and God sent it in answer to her humble and faithful prayer, and her reliance on the promise which was made by an Elder of Christ. A similar experience occurred to me at Koroira, at which village I found an old man named Eagles. Years before he had lived in Salt Lake with his family; but his wife and children grew dissatisfied, and, in fact, apostatized. They departed for New Zealand, and the old brother followed them away from Salt Lake in the hope to bring them back into the Church, and induce them to return to Zion. But his effort had been in vain; and now he was old and fast failing and was the object of their contempt and persecution. They refused to permit him to observe, even in the simplest matters, the religion to which he was honestly and irrevocably devoted. I had heard that there was such a man in the neighborhood, though I had not seen him, and one day when I was passing along the road I met him. I knew that it was he at once. I called him by name, and then explained that I was a "Mormon" Elder from Utah. Brother Eagles expressed great gladness and soon told me his troubles. I asked:

"You came away without any counsel?"

He responded that he had left Utah without counsel; although he had made two or three vain efforts to get a conference with President Young. But he confessed that he had been in too great a hurry; and that it had been a bitter misfortune for him that he had ever left Utah without having counseled with the proper authorities and learned the right thing for him to do.

"I was a Sunday school teacher in Huntsville, and I labored on the Temple Block in Salt Lake; and there among the Saints I was well respected—but here I am treated like a dog. I am very sorrowful and unhappy."

I saw that he was wearied and despondent, and I said to him:

"Never mind, Brother Eagles. Do not feel bad about your troubles. The Lord is looking down upon you in mercy. He sees your afflictions, and He will soon release you. I am very sorry that you came without counsel; but you will be rewarded for the faith that you have had and the labors you have performed."

He answered me that he really hoped the Lord would soon release him, for his burden was very heavy.

We parted and I walked away; and after traveling a short distance I felt a sudden regret that I had spoken to the old gentleman in this way. I thought to myself that he would feel bad, and my words might increase his despondency. I turned around to look for him, and I saw that he had mounted nearly to the crest of a hill, and that he had stopped by the roadside and was leaning upon his stick. The loneliness and the unhappiness of the old man came fully to my mind. I thought to go back and recall what I had said; but the moment I started towards him the voice of the Spirit came to me distinctly, saying:

"Proceed with your journey. Let the old man alone."

I went to Alfred Forest, but returned a few days later; and on my return to Christchurch I called at the post office. The first letter I received was from a friend at Koroira. He stated that on the Monday following my conversation with Brother Eagles the old man had taken to his bed. He had not seemed to suffer any bodily pain, nor to be afflicted in mind. He quietly sank away, apparently in perfect peace and contentment, until the following Saturday, when he died.

After nearly two years of labor in New Zealand, I was preparing to return home. My release was expected every mail. I had not the money with which to pay my fare from Christchurch even to Auckland; but I knew that the way would open and I trusted the Lord implicitly. I had been directed to proceed northward and perform my final labors in the region of Wellington and Hawkes Bay, and I needed the means with which to perform this labor. The Saints in the vicinity of Christchurch were poor. Besides, they had just assisted one missionary with the means to carry him home, and I could neither ask anything, nor were they in a position to give.

The last Sunday but one before I was to start northward, I preached in Christchurch on the restoration of the gospel. One listener was a man named Brownrigg, who was not a member of the Church. He was a man of considerable means and a Catholic.

A day or two later I went up the country a short distance to bid the folks farewell, and then returned to Christchurch. I found that in the meantime Mr. Brownrigg had become Brother Brownrigg, having requested and received baptism at the hands of the Elders during my absence.

On the last Sunday of my stay in that region I again preached in Christchurch and bore my testimony to the assem-

bled Saints.   Brother Brownrigg was there—an attentive listener.   The next day he called me into his business establish-
ment and told me that he had been converted by the sermon
which I had preached on the restoration of the gospel.   He
enquired what my means were, and when I answered that I
was without money, he said:

"You cannot travel without means.   Here are five pounds
for you.   This amount will help you some."

On the following Friday (the day before I was to start away)
he again called me into his store, and this time presented me
with an additional sum of three pounds—making a total of
eight pounds, or $40, which he had given me within a week.

This circumstance impressed me very seriously.   There was
not a Saint in that mission who was able to give me the money
needed for my journey until Brownrigg became a member of
the Church; and he was so quick and generous with his gift
that I was enabled to sail on the day appointed, without any
further trouble or annoyance.   But if I were impressed at this
time, imagine my feeling when I learned shortly after that no
sooner was I gone than Mr. Brownrigg apostatized, and called
the whole system of the gospel "a pack of nonsense!"   I then
felt ready to admit that I had converted Mr. Brownrigg by the
sermon on the restoration of the gospel; because if the Lord
had converted him, he would not have been so ready to deny
the truth.   I do not like to call such a sordid matter as this a
miracle, and yet it seems little short of miraculous that this
man should have come into the Church, have given me the
money necessary for the fulfillment of the Lord's direction to
me—and then have apostatized.   He was a Catholic and
would not have given me the money without joining the
Church.

I reached Auckland in due time; and on the last Sunday in
June, 1880, I preached in Orange Hall, in Newton, Auckland,
my farewell sermon in the Australasian Mission.   I was greatly
moved in delivering this final message of truth; and in the
course of my address I bore a sincere testimony to the truth
of the gospel, and then the spirit prompted me to give to the
people assembled a solemn warning.   I said:

"Other Elders will come to you; but you shall reject their testimony as you now reject mine. But after that, and before six years shall pass away other testimonies will be sent by the Almighty, which you can neither reject nor gainsay. These testimonies will be the testimonies of earthquakes and famines and pestilence; and they will continue to afflict you until but few of you shall live."

While uttering these words I felt so strongly impressed, so confident of their truth, that I told the people to write my utterance down, and watch for its fulfillment. But when I had finished and the Spirit had left me to my own thoughts, I felt almost horrified at the nature of the prophecy which I had almost unconsciously made. I felt my humility and my weakness most vividly, and I also felt almost ashamed, and certainly very fearful concerning the fulfillment of what I had said. That feeling of doubt and almost anger with myself came upon me during the years following, whenever the subject recurred to my mind.

In June, 1886, I received a visit from a brother who had recently come from New Zealand. We were talking about the experiences of my mission, and I said to him:

"It is now just six years since I left Auckland on my return."

No sooner were the words uttered than there flashed through my mind a recollection of the strange prediction which the Spirit had uttered through my lips in Orange Hall; and I thought to myself: "I must have been misled. I have watched the papers carefully, and there is no sign of any such disaster as that which I predicted. If those people did as I requested—if they wrote down the prophecy as it was uttered, some of them now will say, 'There is a falsehood which a Mormon Elder told.'"

This thing worried me for a week, but before ten days had elapsed I saw by the newspapers that a few days before the term of six years had expired a mighty and destructive earthquake occurred at Lake Rotomahana. The effects of this earthquake had been to sink the famous pink terraces of Lake Rotomahana; to substitute for the lake itself a mud volcano and five or six vomiting volcanoes sending forth streams of mud, dust, hot water and other debris which covered the country round about for miles in every direction to a prodigious depth; to destroy lives and to extinguish one village with most of its inhabitants.

I sailed from Auckland on the steamer *Zealandia*, on the 28th day of June, 1880. On this ship I had the pleasure of rejoining my dear friend and companion Elder May, from whom I had been so long separated. He was on his way home from Australia bringing with him a family of Saints.

On board the *Zealandia* were three members of the new South Wales commission, who were going to England on political business. They were, Hon. Alexander Campbell, Captain St. John and another whose name I did not obtain. Mr. Campbell was a gentleman of great suavity of demeanor, fine appearance and wonderful intelligence and information. As soon as he found that "Mormons" were on board he became deeply interested in them. In conversation with us he said:

"I have given some study to your question for the last thirty years. I have watched the course of your people; and I am satisfied that you are working out great social problems. To grapple with these problems successfully has been puzzling to the wisest of statesmen for centuries. I am not one of those who look with contempt upon people who profess strange beliefs. I understand that your community is largely composed of the Anglo-Saxon race; and I know that you cannot find a place on the face of the earth where an enduring community of this kind has been built up for the purposes of lust. Your enemies say that this is your motive, but I am convinced to the contrary. The Anglo-Saxons never descend to that. When they unite in great movements they have a grand object in view."

A few days later when we were crossing the line he came from the cabin with a newspaper in his hand, sat down alongside of me, and said: ·

"Mr. Shreeve, I understand from your jubilee report that you have about 50,000 children enrolled in your Sabbath School Union?"

I answered, "Yes sir—I believe that is about the number."

He said, then, "Do you know if these children are trained aright that you have growing up in your mountain community a power which the world has not seen since Adam stepped out of the Garden of Eden? I assure you that it is so. These children have not the tradition of ages to combat, but their minds are unhampered and pure, and you can mould them to the fulfillment of a great purpose. I repeat it, you have growing up with these children a power which the world has not seen since father Adam stepped out of the Garden of Eden."

Mr. Campbell stopped a brief time in San Francisco; and had intended to make a lengthy stay in order to be in Salt Lake on the occasion of the grand celebration to be given there on Pioneer's Day. He succeeded in reaching our beloved city in time, and he was an admiring witness of the exercises in which thousands of the young Saints participated. Mr. Campbell watched with sparkling eyes, and he drew a long breath as he said to a companion: "My friend, the half of this people's greatness has not been told."

———

I reached my home in July, of the year 1880. Only returning Elders can understand my joy. By the favor of God I had been enabled to perform my duty; and every blessing pronounced upon my head had been literally fulfilled.

I would not to-day exchange the experience and the Helpful Visions of my mission for the wealth of the world.

TRAITORS.

Solemn Warnings - A Traitor can Never be
Anything but Despicable - Examples
of the Past.

By Ben E. Rich.

THE traitor is the moral cannibal.   He feasts on the
mental worth, the social reputation, the political welfare and
the earthly life of his trusting and betrayed friend.   He is the
human serpent, which nurses and revives at the fire of char-
ity, and then darts his strengthened venom at the bosom of
his benefactor.   What the grub is to the heart of oak, the
gnawing rat to the ship's timbers, the flaw to the diamond,
the poisonous asp to the sheltering flower—all that, aye, and
more, is the traitor to mankind.   No cause is so sacred, no
being is so exalted as to be free from the pollution of his
betraying touch.   Even the celestial legions had their arch-
traitor.   Earth, from the day of Eden, has never been free
from his treacherous kiss.   Since the hour when man first
learned to owe allegiance to his fellow-man, profane, rebellious
betrayers have worked their insidious way, like devastating
worms, through all the pillars upholding holy men and noble
causes.

The traitor is the worst of all thieves; for he steals sacred
freedom from his trusting associates.   The traitor is the worst
of all murderers; for he plunges the assassin's knife into the
back of his believing friend.

Two soldiers are standing at the picket post—in the dark night, the silent forest. They are sworn and trusted comrades. The army of the foe surges around them; and they know that ghastly death is grinning at them from every glade which opens from the dark center to the blacker depths beyond, and whispering to them upon every wind that stirs the odorous branches. But they fear no blow from a foeman's shaft—that noble death is but the chance of war. Secure in mutual confidence, they tremble not. They speak of country, home; of wives and little, prattling babes. And yet, while the words of soft, pathetic love arc on the lips of one, the other plunges a traitorous knife, hilt-deep, into a friendly, loyal heart. And then the assassin sweeps like the shadow of a lost soul over the face of the betrayed sentinel; he creeps across tender moss and between the trunks of mighty trees—everywhere leaving the crimson, accusing stain—until he reaches a distant camp-fire; and at the feet of the waiting enemy he lays down his reeking knife and takes his purse of gold. This is the traitor. And when the moon comes up, stealing amidst the rustling leaves, he looks upon the cold, white face of a betrayed friend, whose last word was of confident love told to the ear of a hired assassin.

Two men are joined in a patriotic cause. To the maintenance of the principle of just freedom they pledge their lives, their fortunes and their sacred honor. History will call the men who arc true to this cause loyal and brave. The tyrant whom they seek to overthrow calls them conspirators. They meet in a darkened room, with curtains closely drawn. Soft mats hush the sound of the firm footfall. Stern voices, more used to the vast circumference of the field or the resonant heights of the forum, are stilled to a woman's whisper. These two men are meeting to sign and yield to each other, for distant comrades, the pledge of mutual fidelity. The one who is master of the house places his guest at a table and spreads before him for final execution the plans of insurrection, the lists of friends and confederates, the oaths of reciprocal fealty. As the visitor attaches his name to the solemn instruments, he sighs and says:

"Oh, trusted friend! I yield to this cause not only my life, my fortune and my sacred honor; but I pledge to it and to the integrity of you and our allies my sweet wife and my only son —both at once my present pride and future joy!"

While the words are uttered, the bold and noble hand traces its way in affirmatory signature across parchment and paper. Scarcely has the thrilling whisper of the patriot ceased to agitate the damask curtains, when the hangings are parted by the vulture hand of the other conspirator; and between their open folds steal the soldiers of the tyrant. These warlike hands grasp the shoulders of the patriot; and as they drag him forth to dungeon and to death, the betraying host cries:

"Bind him fast, lest he should escape and slay me!"

The coward, muffled in a cloak, soon steals from the sombre chamber to the palace of the minister and lays before that waiting officer his trophies of broken plans and fatal lists. He gets in return his patent of rank, his gift of confiscated estates, his pledge of his personal security. This is the traitor. And when the sun of the third day shall rise, its first pitying beams will fall upon the gory block, the black executioner, the basket with its dread burden, and the headless trunk of the patriot whose trust and hope had been in a false friend.

Two men are joined with others in proclaiming an unpopular but holy doctrine. Hand in hand they go through the earth testifying to men, to cities, to nations, the mighty truths. They say to all lands and to all peoples:

"We know that this is the living, burning truth. God has spoken from the heavens, and we are His witnesses."

To each other—in all the sacred friendliness of long association, of missionary labor, and of a communion together when every human law and hand seemed against them—they speak in faithful hope of the glorious cause which they espouse, and of the divine necessity which they are under to be faithful to God and their brethren. Their views are not in accord with public sentiment and suddenly they are dragged before a cruel tribunal and charged that they are teaching crime. But the law of the land says: "No man shall be punished because of his sincere religious views or practices." And the judge before whom they are arraigned calls to them:

"Continue to declare that ye are doing the will of God, and in prison ye shall rest. But acknowledge that ye are proclaiming a man-made system, and pledge that ye will cease, and ye shall go free."

And one of them who are arraigned says:

"Oh, judge! I acknowledge thy supremacy. I will obey thy law. I will not advise others to break it. So long as thou and thy masters shall command, I will worship the graven image."

And then he takes his seal of amnesty, bought at the price of a people's freedom, and creeps from the presence of the court a man—nay, a creature—inviolable of his fellows, but haunted ever by the shadow of Judas. This is the traitor.

And when the other prisoner is arraigned he cries:

"This is my religion! God gave it to me! Ye may take my earthly life, but ye cannot sap my manhood nor strang'e my conscience."

Then the judge, who has a mission to learn if these people are sincere, answers to the prisoner and for the far-off masters of the court:

"Thou canst not come within the law; because thou canst not claim sincerity. Thy brother and fellow-laborer hath just now recanted, and this is proof that thou art not sincere, but wickedly obstinate. If thy brother had with thee remained firm and immovable I might have believed in thy cause. But what man hath done man can do again. Therefore, recant or rest thou within the cold and lonely walls."

And the sun and moon of another month, stealing through iron-bound chinks of rock, see the patriot pacing a dismal cell.

The traitor calls himself a reformer. He is merely a coward. And of all the wretches whose presence taints the air of earth and heaven, the coward is the worst. Great Cæsar said:

"The coward's fears make him die many times before his death.

"The valiant never taste of death but once.

"Of all the wonders that I yet have heard, it seems to me most strange that men should fear seeing that death, a necessary end, will come when it will come."

The traitor professes to believe that his act of betrayal will disrupt the cause which he deserts. This is the coward rebel's wish. How abjectly and miserably he fails! Sometimes the traitor lops from the sturdy trunk a straggling branch; but does the tree thrive less for that? Nay. The other twigs only bear blossoms the more redolent and fruit the more rosy. Sometimes the traitor tears away a cracked, a seamed, a shaling stone from the half-completed structure. What if a measure of disaster follow? Cannot the builder renew? And does he not choose better rock to bear the weight of his fair edifice? Sometimes the traitor only hastens the success which he seeks to avert; sometimes he delays the triumph against which he rebels. But always ultimately the car of destiny moves to its appointed end. And the cowardly betrayer who thought to stop its career by holding back with his puny arms is dragged by it to his miserable end, while his associates—dead or alive go with it to the day of triumph.

THERE was once a man of mighty prowess, endowed from his first breath with a wondrous strength. When he grew to manhood, brutes, men and even armies fell in the dust at his feet. It had been divinely promised of him that he should be a marvel of strength, and that he should begin to deliver Israel out of the hands of the Philistines, and men and chains, and bolts and gates could not prevail against his manly, heroic lustiness. But there came a woman, with her soft, betraying touch. She caressed him and begged for love of her that he would reveal the secret of his miraculous strengh. In a foolish moment he yielded; and then were his Jove-like locks shorn from his head; and he became a blind lackey, the serf of the Philistines. Delilah, the betrayer, with her traitorous kiss upon Samson's lips, and her traitorous whisper through the tent to his waiting enemy, could do what no thousand of open foes could accomplish. She made the proud, superb, perfect lion a weak, whining whelp.

A MIGHTY king had a well-beloved son to whom he had given and forgiven more than is usually bestowed upon one of human kind. And yet the son traitorously plotted the downfall and even the murder of his royal sire, and the usurpation of the throne. He might have succeeded in his cruel, parricidal treason, but that he himself was in turn betrayed and finally slain. And when the grand, great-hearted, poetic monarch learned that Absalom, the sweet, the beautiful, the dearly-beloved, was dead, he wept before all Israel, and as he went his sorrowful way thus he said:

"O, my son Absalom! My son, my son Absalom! Would God I had died for thee, O, Absalom, my son, my son!"

If that arrow-pierced heart of the betraying and betrayed Absalom could have quickened but for one moment, how much sharper than the physical death-thrust would it have felt King David's cry of infinite forgiveness! But the past was irrevocable. Israel's lordly king, the beloved of God, was moaning in anguish at the gate of the city; and the beautiful Absalom, with the fatal hair, the beloved of his royal sire, was lying dead in the pit in the deserted wood, with ignoble stone crushing his lifeless body.

War, murder, exile were powerless to bring such desolation to these royal hearts; but when Absalom, the forgiven murderer, became a betrayer infinite woe fell around the name of the dead prince and the bowed head of the living king. But though the great tenderness of the psalmist could compass remission for the crime of Absalom, the nation and history must be more harsh. When a subject, for self-agrandizement, rises against a king, he is a traitor; but he is a thrice-damned traitor when that monarch against whom he rebels is his own father.

WOMEN are often false to their lovers; subjects to their sovereigns, and even sons to their sires. Divinity itself is no invulnerable shield against betrayal. A merciful Christ came to save mankind from torment and lift them into eternal radiance. He chose and trusted His apostles. He ministered to them and with them. They each could give a testimony that

their Master was the anointed Savior, the Son of the living
God.　Persecution came upon Him like the storm cloud low-
ers upon the snowy mountain and enfolded Him in a gloomy
embrace.　The prospect of suffering with this God-like Master, whom he had served as purse-bearer when the danger was
not great, made Judas weak unto betrayal.　Cowardice and
avarice worked together in the traitor heart.　He kissed and
cried:

"Master, master! Hail, master!"

Then he took his thirty pieces of silver; and with them he
accepted a hatred of all mankind.

The compassionate Redeemer of the world hung upon the
cruel cross with drops of agony upon His radiant brow, while
his lips were wreathed in a pained but forgiving smile.　And
Judas, the traitor, already tasting the infernal torments, called
in vain to stay the progress of his dread act.　The black-hearted
deed was done.　The mocking trial had passed, sentence had
been pronounced and executed; and then the betrayer groaned
and flung the money from him as a sinful, burning thing which
had no worth.　Upon the bloody field he cast himself and his
bowels gushed forth in useless contrition.　He died upon the
spot which his blood-money purchased for the burial of strangers and criminals in the land.

A BRILLIANT general fell into disgrace with his military
superiors and with the civil government of his country.　He
was impetuous and impatient of restraint.　He was proud
even to arrogance; he was extravagant even to the furthest
limit of honesty.　Other men had been advanced to higher
posts—he felt himself degraded.　His disbursements upon one
of his heroic expeditions were still unsettled—he felt himself
defrauded.　A tyrant foe invested his country and sought to
subjugate her people.　He listened to the voice of ignoble
avarice, of proud passion, of offended arrogance.　With delib-
erate humiliation he sought a place of vast trust among the
defenders of his country.　He was appointed to the command
of a great river fortress—the key to the interior, the storage
house of munitions dearly bought, highly prized and abso-

lutely necessary for the repulse of the invaders. He sold his rank, his honor and his interest in his native land. Just at the hour when his bargain was to be decided, his old friend and admirer, the noble commander-in-chief, said to him:

"My dear Arnold, I am now forming my army for active operations in the field. I want a fighting general. Come, I offer you the command of the left wing, at once the post of danger and of honor."

The traitor's face flushed with shame. He pleaded an old wound as reason why he should not go into the battle-field. Then he went to meet Andre and give the last assurance to his British masters that he was theirs, body and soul. By the interposition of America's sublime destiny his plot was discovered and foiled.

Arnold, the traitor, crept away to escape a betrayer's death. He received his British uniform, his British gold, his British sword. He even came back with his mercenary horde to ravage, burn, destroy the little town in Connecticut where first he saw the light.

Years later, the great Frenchman, Talleyrand, met a distinguished-looking man at an English country inn. The two gentlemen were total strangers to each other; but they soon engaged in conversation upon the great question of Democracy. When they were about to part, Talleyrand said to his companion:

"From your knowledge of all that relates to the United States, I am sure that you must be an American; my name is Talleyrand, and I am about to visit that country; perhaps you will be kind enough to give me letters of introduction to some of your friends there."

When the illustrious diplomat had finished his request, the other gentleman bowed low; and when he looked up his face, even to his lips, was gray as a-hes. In a voice which sounded weird and cheerless as the moan of a November wind across a deserted marsh, he answered:

"Yes, I am an American. I was born in America. I have spent nearly all my life there. But I am probably the only American living who can say, 'I have not one friend in my native land.' No, not one. Sir, I am Benedict Arnold."

Talleyrand turned away from Arnold with a shudder, while the miserable traitor crept silently from the room.

When the unhappy wretch was dying in the midst of contempt and poverty he grew delirious. At the last moment of his ruined life he called to the devoted wife who had been the sharer of all his woe:

"Bring to me, I beg you, the epaulettes and sword knots which Washington gave me. Let me die in my old American uniform, the uniform in which I fought my battles. May my God forgive me for ever having worn any other!"

THE greatest army which the world ever saw was gathered at Thermopylæ more than two thousand years ago.

This was the Persian host assembled to do battle to the little band of Spartans. So intrepidly did the Greeks defend that sacred defile which gave entrance to their beloved land that Xerxes became out of all hope of forcing his way through the Spartan ranks. This was the moment for the traitor. Before the proud Xerxes could withdraw his myriads, the betrayer came—a Greek, a native of the sublime country. With servile words he flung himself at the feet of the gorgeous Persian. He offered to lead the invaders to an eminence overlooking the heroic defenders of Greece. His coward wish was granted; and when the next morning dawned Leonidas and his followers saw the spears and helmets of their foes flashing at them from the heights.

The rest is the most sublime tragedy of profane history.

And the traitor who betrayed the noblest souls of Greece to their death received his gold and precious stones. He might have died in the honest obscurity in which he was born and reared, but for his coward act.

Ah! such notoriety is purchased at too high a price. It would be better for a man to stand modestly and firmly before his country's foe; to fall unrecognized and without praise; to fill a grave over which the words shall stand cut into ineffaceable granite, "An unknown soldier, who died in defense of his country." Ah, yes! far better thus to fall and fill an unknown grave—to be unremembered forevermore of men—than to win a name of infamy, to fill the pages of history and be recollected of all human-kind while men shall hate a traitor.

A PROPHET of Almighty God came in the full sunlight of this great nineteenth century to lead men back to the glory of their Creator. His open enemies sought his life; but for years their murderous effort was in vain. He continued his sacred ministry upon the earth, with a power which was divine, until the hour for the traitorous kiss. When Bennett sinned and then through hate betrayed, the shadows of martyrdom began closing around our grand Prophet and Patriarch. When the Laws and the Higbees, the Fosters and the Cowles, became traitors and gave their efforts to aid the assassin persecutors of their sworn brother and leader; then, indeed, was the fate of Joseph and Hyrum sealed.

A governor of a sovereign State betrayed them to a cruel death; and Carthage repeated the divine tragedy of Calvary. The Prophet and Patriarch have passed to their glorious immortality; their names shall fill a thousand hymns of praise on earth and welcome in the heavens. But the traitors—miserable reptiles—will be scorned through countless ages.

It is always the same—prince or peasant, apostle or soldier —if a man be a traitor he is remembered for that and nothing more. If his station be lowly, he will seek in vain to hide his shame in his native obscurity; for it will burst forth in lurid, bloody letters to the sight of all the ages that shall come. If his station be exalted he may try and try again, but vainly, to cover his treason with the glory of his rank or wealth; for it will blacken all his brilliance and leave his place a plague spot; his fame, a grinning skeleton of dead despair; his career, an undying infamy.

But whatever may be the varied circumstances and results attending the wretched lives of traitors, there is this lesson which all humanity may draw: Successful or unsuccessful in their treason, betrayers are always execrated; successful or unsuccessful in their treason, they always live long enough to repent; successful or unsuccessful in their treason, they may never in this life know a waking moment when their own coward fears do not make them doubt the fidelity of every soul about them; successful or unsuccessful in their earthly treason, when they shall stand in that other world face to face with their betrayed friends, they will know that the blackest of all offenders are *cowardly*, assassin traitors.

At that great day Judas Iscariot will not be the only traitor to cry:

"It had been good for me that I had not been born!"

Every crisis at every period and with every nation exposes traitors just as it exalts to view patriots.

This Church has seen at every critical point of its career, the betrayer as well as the savior springing to the front. The present emergency with the people of Utah is no exception to this rule.

Just as there are men sacrificing comfort and earthly prosperity to the cause, and men who are willing to give life itself to defend God's work from the attacks of its enemies; so there are people who will sell their own sacred heritage and the freedom of the community, for wealth, popularity or personal safety.

And more than this—the people are surrounded by men placed here to represent the government who are false to every trust, and whose opposition can be estimated in dollars or coerced by bigotry.

We have some traitors to ourselves within our homes; we have more traitors to truth and justice outside our walls.

Less than two thousand years ago the great Roman republic was at the zenith of its power. Some of the free and enterprising citizens of that mighty land emigrated into the cold, mountainous regions of the north and established a colony which they called Beville. They set up the Roman standard, and claimed the territory in the name of their country.

After overcoming untold difficulties, they sent messengers to Rome asking for recognition; and saying that, inasmuch as they had given a grand, rich domain to their beloved mother land, they should be placed upon an equal footing with their free-born fellow-citizens. But the politicians at Rome would not listen to this request; and Beville was kept in the vassalage of a conquered province.

All the governors, judges and many of the local officers were sent from some other part of the republic; and they treated the people of Beville with the most dreadful severity, while they dispatched to Rome the most vicious and cruelly false reports concerning the honest citizens of the province or colony unto which they had been sent to govern and to judge. Many of them were most contemptible knaves and traitors. They once had a governor who traitorously violated his oath to give a certificate of election to a man who had one vote in a dozen, and whose only claim to consideration was his wealth and willingness to make loans on desperate political titles; a governor who deprived a good public unsectarian university of its needed support and then declared that the people of Beville opposed education; a governor who broke his plighted word in order that he might leave upon the fair land the espionage of an unjust and unaccountable commission; a governor who basely betrayed the consul that maintained him in office by saying with egotism which is bleached white with concentrated lye: "I wrote all of such and such portions of the consul's message;" a governor who was called a thief upon the floor of the Senate; a governor who had a list of wildcat, highway-robbery mining stocks which bore his name and title—all for sale under the glare and glamor of his civil position; a governor whose brains were rattling chestnuts, whose heart was infinitesimal, bearing proof that a single atom 'can exist, and whose beauty—his only virtue—was that of the painted harlot and the whitened sepulchre.

Then they had one judge, a man who should now be where Deacon Bitters was supposed to be years ago—measuring sulphur to make orthodox hell fire; a judge whose class-meeting morality was so dreadfully shocked by an advocate's grand conduct that the advocate was disbarred from practice because he refused to cast off and make a wanderer of the wife who had loved and honored him, and who had borne him sweet, confiding children; a judge who could then send lechers forth from his court crowned with bay and laurel and bearing their

edicts of license in their hands; a judge who practically said
to the libertine, "Go your way rejoicing.   Prey upon virtue
without stint.   Bring ruin into your own home, and then
spread disease and deadly desolation wherever else you can
gain an entrance.   You are free to come and go.   My thun-
derbolts of justice, forged at the fire of fanaticism and fanned
by the wind of protection for my own son, all these shafts are
for our over-scrupulous opponents, the people of Beville;" a
judge whose brain was honeycombed with the devious turn-
ings of treacherous thoughts, whose heart was an icicle, and
whose alleged moral desire—his only virtue—was the great
enfolding cloak which could cover every prostitute and para-
mour in the land.

THEY had another judge: a creature whose miserable physical appearance was but the photograph of the horrid, ugly
soul within; a judge who was willing to slay women and children, and to tread over their corpses to gain his nomination; a
judge who became known within one brief year as an infamous
wretch, who practiced cruelty with most Satanic ingenuity; a
judge whose brain was a tape-worm lie, with five hundred
self-sustaining and specie-propagating joints.   Whose heart
was a pain in his stomach caused by a vacuum, and whose
ability to sermonize, his only virtue, was an adulterous union
of vanity and falsehood.

THESE men were all traitors—traitors to God, to their country
and to the parents who vainly tried to endow them with manhood.

But to-day we in Utah have a few traitors a little nearer
home.   There are men who say:

"I once loved the cause well enough to die for it; but now I
hate the work and the people, because a leading man once did
me an injury.   I will become an informer."

There are still others—the careless traitors—the men and
women who cover their thoughtless treason with a joke, and
clothe unmeant betrayal with a smile.   These are the people
who learn the sacred secrets of a friend, a brother, and then

tattle the forbidden words here, there and everywhere. And when the careless gossip reaches the ears of our persecutors—as it does all too often—it becomes, not friendly joking, but a stern, almost tragic accusation. And when the victim is brought to sad disaster, the very people who have helped the wicked betrayal are among the first to say:

"I am not surprised that he should come to grief; he is so careless. The great wonder is that it did not happen before, because everybody has been talking about his affairs."

: Ah! to-day we see Delilah who betrays her husband; and Absalom, who is traitorous to his father; and Judas, who is traitorous to his father; and Judas, who would betray his master for gold or popular approval; the Arnold who says, "It is a losing cause, and I may as well desert while there is yet time."

Yes, there are cowards and traitors in the land. Well, let there be, then, since such are necessary to make the sum of human existence—let them live as hyenas do.

Grand Harry the V., of England—superb, glorious Harry—stood once upon the shore of France with his little band of soldiers to face the countless legions of his hereditary foe. He heard a murmur as of fear; and turning to his nobles he looked at them from flashing.eyes and spoke these very significant words:

> "He which hath no stomach to this fight,
> Let him depart, his passport shall be made,
> And crowns for convoy put into his purse:
> We would not die in that man's company,
> That fears his fellowship to die with us.
> I speak not this as doubting any here!
> For, did I but suspect a fearful man,
> He should have leave to go away betimes;
> Lest, in our need, he might infect another,
> And make him of like spirit to himself.
> If any such be here, as God forbid !
> Let him depart, before we need his help."

www.ingramcontent.com/pod-product-compliance
Lightning Source LLC
Chambersburg PA
CBHW021410090426
42742CB00009B/1094